Angels
THE LIFTING OF THE VEIL

Angels
THE LIFTING OF THE VEIL

Thomas Keller
and Deborah S. Taylor

HAMPTON ROADS
PUBLISHING COMPANY, INC.

Illustrations and cover design
by John Wadsworth, Wadsworth Alliance

For information write:

Hampton Roads Publishing Company, Inc.
134 Burgess Lane
Charlottesville, VA 22902

Or call: (804) 296-2772
FAX: (804) 296-5096

If you are unable to order this book from your local
bookseller, you may order directly from the publisher.
Quantity discounts for organizations are available.
Call 1-800-766-8009, toll-free.

10 9 8 7 6 5 4 3

ISBN 1-878901-96-6

Printed on acid-free paper in the United States of America

Dedicated
to

Laine Schroeder, age 14
and
Marianne Olivieri, age 15

Two joyful and wonderful angels
who in their passing
lifted the veil for many.

Table of Contents

We acknowledge:

The One Source of all that is, The Angelic Kingdom, Living Love, Living Truth, and the potential of Life;

Amy Davis, for her tireless translation of Thomas's lecture tapes, her enthusiasm for the project, and her heart-felt, loving support;

Alma Pendergast, Colin and Marlene George, Wayne and Doris Miller, and Wayne Jennings, who provided us with the funds, without which this book would not have been possible;

Bess Cutter, whose profound wisdom and healing encouraged and inspired us throughout the project and kept us always focused on the goal;

Flo Calhoun and "The Nameless Ones," whose vision of the future of Earth and humankind expanded our awareness and confidence in the Divine Plan;

John Wadsworth, our beloved photographer and partner, for his unconditional friendship and his creative vision that was truly a gift from the angels;

Timothy Paul Keller, for "I experience what I express" and "It's just an experience";

Tara Ann Keller, for constantly asking, "Is the book done?";

Jesse Seymour, whose joyful presence during the project was a gift to Deborah's soul that showed her that dreams do indeed come true when you call on the angels for help with those you love;

Paul Ricioppo, whose belief in the angels helped make this book possible;

Randolph Williams, whose consistent support over the past decade helped Deborah to live the dream;

Bruce Shelton, for his spirited willingness to cover for Thomas at the Center so more time could be given to the book;

The Fellowship Family and all who said "Just do it";

Hampton Roads Publishing for believing in us from start to finish and Kathy Grotz, whose skillful editing helped refine and deepen our vision;

MaryAnna Keller, who has always supported Thomas's relationship with the Angelic Kingdom; and

Jon Robertson, at A.R.E. Press, whose initial support and guidance allowed us to begin the book.

Chapter One

A Journey With the Angels

Dearly Beloved,
The veil is now lifting; the time is ripe for the fulfillment
of your greatest dreams. We, the Angelic Kingdoms, stand
poised with messages of great joy, waiting only for your
permission to respond with assistance. Let this time be your
time—this joy your joy—for it is your divine birthright to
live and move and have your being in the Kingdom of
Heaven, as the child of the Source from which you are and
forever will be.

The Angels

W hen I was five years old, I was asleep one night on the screened-in porch of our house on Long Island Sound, when I was startled awake by a flash of light. When I opened my eyes, above me an angel hovered in midair, dressed in the most beautiful colors I had ever seen. In her tiny, perfectly-shaped hand she held a wand that lit my bed with light and bathed me in an overwhelming feeling of love I can remember to this day.

For Thomas, the angels appeared while presenting a lecture on self-love to a gathering in Virginia Beach. Before he began, he sat alone praying that God would send the angels to assist him. When the workshop began, he was shocked to hear himself saying things he didn't know he knew. In fact, it occurred to him that if whoever was sending the information decided to stop, he'd be forced to end his talk mid-sentence since he had no idea where he was going or where he would end up. Even more astonishing was that, as the lecture continued, each time a member of the audience would *think* of a question, Thomas would instantly "hear" it in his mind and respond with an answer before the question was ever asked. When the workshop ended, a line of people formed to shake his hand; some reported seeing angels, some said they had heard them. Others called him later to tell him that his talk had changed their lives.

Little did either of us know that these isolated experiences would mark the beginning of years of celestially-inspired miracles which would cause us to come to know the Angelic Kingdom as companions and eventually friends. When they finally drew us together to write this book, we had each privately made a decision to tell our own angel stories; yet, although we were friends at the time, neither of us knew of the other's decision until one unusually warm day in early April in Virginia Beach as I stood browsing through a stack of angel books at a local bookstore. As I scanned the shelves, I suddenly *knew* it was time to write about my angel experiences. When I returned home, I called Thomas, a minister at a local church, and asked him if he'd like to collaborate. After a long silence, he cleared his throat and, voice shaking, informed me that the day before he had been down on his knees in the sanctuary asking the angels for help so that he could finally write the angel book he too had long dreamed of writing. Once the decision was made, the details fell magically into place. Money came in the form of contributions from friends as far away as Canada. A wonderful friend offered to transcribe the endless hours of tapes of our brainstorming sessions, and an internationally-recognized photographer offered to illustrate the book. Perhaps most amazing was that within two months we had an offer from a publisher. As Thomas often said, "It was so easy, it was scary."

Once the commitment was made, the angels began to participate in every aspect of our lives—in our relationships, in our professional lives, even in our sleep. In short, there was no downtime.

We found that when you make a choice to co-create with the Angelic Kingdom—although it's certainly delightful and always full of surprises—it's not child's play. When you give permission to winged things to come into your life, you give permission to be changed—because they *will* come; that is a given, and, when face-to-face with such love and power, it's hard *not* to be changed.

But change was not a particularly welcome prospect for either of us, despite our best intentions and our dreams, especially when it meant confronting the sobering realization that if we weren't willing to make the commitment to live the truths the angels conveyed, we may as well not begin.

Clearly, this was the wrestling with the angels spoken of in the Biblical story of Jacob; we too wrestled with winged things as we were forced to dig down deep and consider long and hard the question of why, after all, we were writing this book and if we were actually willing to *experience* what was given, knowing as we did that all our endless ramblings on the subject of the angels didn't amount to much if we couldn't reap a significant amount of joy in the process.

It was not easy. At every turn, our deepest, darkest fears rose to the surface, threatening to block our every effort. For me, it was a constant leap of faith as each morning, awkward and flat-footed with sweaty palms and endless doubts, I would sit before the blank page and wait to hear the still, small voice of inspiration, praying it would offer some hint as to where we were going and how, in heaven's name, we might get there.

For Thomas, there was the endless battle with himself as, day after day, he would face a vicious inner critic who would whisper in his ear, "You don't know what you're doing," forever attempting to persuade him that he was simply wasting his time. Some days he was afraid that the angels would have nothing to say or what was said would be trite and boring; other days he feared that what was said was simply a lie—or, even worse—what if it *were* the truth? What would the consequences be if he were to choose to heed the celestial messages and actually allow the angels to accompany him in every moment of his daily life?

Still, no matter how often we tried to run from the task, believing there were thousands of infinitely more pressing demands than writing yet another book on angels, eventually, when faced with an impending deadline, we simply had to make a choice to align ourselves with what the angels called *truth,* and make the necessary changes in our lives to allow room for the absolute, every-cell-in-the-body commitment to expressing it. Eventually, this book and the mysterious process of feeling and remembering our way "home" became one and the same. Along the way, we discovered something that changed both our lives; when you ask, you *are* answered; when you knock, the door will be opened and, when it is, the angels are there to assist you, every step of the way.

A Blessing From on High

Beyond our five senses, angelic hosts fill the universe. In their assignment as creative emissaries that express the attributes of God, they are seeking, just as we are, to expand their experience and wisdom through new insights and express—to an ever-greater extent—the qualities of divinity. Angels are the evidence of what we have always hoped the Creator might be like. Legions surround us, wanting only to inspire, guide, protect, and love. They have been sent from above as if to say, "Experience what I *am:* love, peace, wisdom, joy, harmony, and, most of all, life more abundant."

Since the beginning of time, the angels have been available to assist us in remembering our true divine nature. At present, they are awaiting our recognition in order to be of greater service, as collectively we awaken to who we are and why we've come here in the first place. But since they are not permitted to interfere without our invitation, we must first express the willingness to know the truth and give permission for assistance to be given.

Dearly Beloved,
It is our greatest Joy to be with you and assist in all that you might wish to accomplish. Yet if, when you are about your work and play, you find yourself saying, "I will do

this," and are blind to us as you attempt to fulfill your desires, we are helpless to assist. But if, before you begin your expression, you ask the Father to send His Angels to share in your experience, then listen, for we will be there, standing close to guide the hand and whisper in the ear. Yes, we will be a part as surely as you call, for you cannot call without our response. We delight to be with you and share in your expression. So, in all things that you do, ask the Father to let us share with you what we see as Living Love. When we share with you in this way, Living Love draws closer to us and closer to you; in the process, we all grow.

The Angels

How We Met the Angels

By tuning your senses to the unseen world and beginning to learn about and experience the Angelic Kingdoms, it is possible to take angels out of the realm of a charming idea and bring them into everyday life as loving companions who know our needs even before we ask. Although, for both Thomas and me, the road has been a long one, today they are just as much an intimate part of our lives as family and friends.

But this was not always the case.

My personal journey began with the recognition of a deep wound that no success and no variety of worldly happiness could ever begin to heal. No matter where I looked and what I experienced, life appeared meaningless and absurd. Eventually, after years of chaos and confusion and finally driven by the sudden onset of a mysterious illness, I entered into what the mystics call a Dark Night of the Soul.

Illness was the initiation, as if to become well I had to become ill. To live, I had to die.

It began more than ten years ago when I awakened one morning feeling an exhaustion that made even the simplest act virtually impossible. Before then, I had been blessed with near-perfect health and was—in truth—somewhat indifferent to it. Yet, from one day to the next, the simple act of breathing became an enormous effort, and day-by-day I watched helplessly as every ounce of strength drained away. Out of work, I spent most of my days propped up in bed; on the rare days when I left, it was only to travel from one doctor to the next in search of a cure. Yet, despite endless medical tests and a staggering number of unpaid bills, none could be found.

In the months that followed, everything—money, a home I loved, and some of my closest friends—was stripped away. Finally, in sheer desperation and on the advice of a friend, I went to see a psychic. That visit marked a turning point; from that moment forward, nothing was ever the same. In the space of a few short hours, a virtual stranger told me things about my life and my most secret dreams no one else could possibly have known. She spoke to me about the purpose of my life and told me I must write a book—many books, in fact—and that, until I did, I would not recover. Not certain whether to laugh or cry, I remember asking sarcastically how in God's name *I* would write a book. Staring dreamily into the distance, she replied, "Don't worry. The angels will help you."

Although her words had a profound effect, the strangest sensation was the recognition that everything that was said I had already known—though I couldn't remember having ever heard it verbalized until that day. Nonetheless, by morning the doubts crept in and for days I lay alone attempting to imagine how, even if my very life depended on it, I would ever have even the foggiest notion of how in heaven's name to write a book. Although I had edited a magazine and religiously kept a journal over the years, I hardly considered myself a writer. The truth is—though I had dreamed of it and often secretly wished for it—when it came time to actually do it, I didn't believe in myself enough to begin.

But the seed was planted, and eventually the helplessness I experienced as I found myself growing weaker by the hour allowed me no choice but to entertain, if only briefly, the possibility that what was conveyed might actually be the truth. Finally, one particularly grueling night, as I was propped up on pillows and struggling to breathe, something snapped. I simply stopped resisting. The next morning, quite without premeditation and with an ease I would never have imagined, I wrote—poured out my heart onto the empty white pages. When I finished and climbed into bed to read what was written, I was shocked—not only did it actually make sense, but I had no idea where it had come from. Later that same night, for the first time in nearly four months, I slept soundly. Little did I know that that day would mark the beginning of a strange sort of apprenticeship with winged things that would alter the course of my life forever.

One year later, I had completed a novel about a writer who takes a cabin on an island off the coast of Greece to recover from a mysterious illness and discovers that, as she writes, angels whisper in her ear. In the process, not only did I regain my health, but I also learned to write. Still, despite endless attempts to find a publisher, the manuscript did not sell. Four years later, having re-written it more than a dozen times, I simply gave up and closed the chapter on a time of my life that I still can't remember without wincing.

But the angels didn't leave my life, even though I had virtually given up on them; before long, I had one of my first "real-life" encounters with the Angelic Kingdom. At the time, having embarked on a study of various healing techniques, I was working as an apprentice to a local healer, although I doubted my ability and was curious more than motivated to ever take it seriously. One day, however, she became violently ill, called me to her side, and asked for help. In that one moment, the only thought that crossed my mind was that I loved her so much that I would do virtually anything to help her recover—even make a complete and utter fool of myself by acting as if I might be able to assist. Over the next few hours, as I silently massaged her body with oil, I had my first vision of the angels. It overturned everything I had ever known. As I worked, the room flooded with light and whole flocks of angels appeared to circle my hands and move through her body each place I laid my hands. Unable to hold back the tears and bursting with a strange kind of joy, I continued in the midst of an almost overwhelming feeling of love that made every day I had ever lived until that moment click neatly into place.

When it was over, she sat up smiling, miraculously recovered; no one was more surprised than I. Over the next few months, the mysterious angelic visions continued and, though at the time I had never touched a paintbrush, I began painting the faces I saw whenever I closed my eyes to pray. Yet, oddly enough, it still didn't occur to me that angels might actually be real.

Finally, in the early '90s, I attended an angel workshop given by Thomas at a nearby church. Although I had never been one to attend workshops and most of what I learned over the years came from books and personal experiences, I was strangely urged, in a dream I had while napping just hours before the workshop was to begin, to go to this particular event. That night, I learned how to call on the angels and in the process realized that, in all my years of writing and painting, I had been calling on them all along; I had simply not been aware of it. Still, it would take another year before I gathered the courage to try again to write a book.

For Thomas, a relationship with the angels came after years of self-hate and self-denial, caught in an endless pattern of drugs and alcohol he used to quiet the confusion and somehow fill the aching void of a life that lacked meaning and purpose:

"As far back as I can remember, I felt as if life had no real meaning. Although my parents and teachers attempted to convey their beliefs and demonstrate how to live a good life, nothing really made any sense to me. School was difficult, to say the least, and, by the time I was in the eighth grade for the second year in a row, I found myself in a situation quite different than that of the other children in my class: 18 years old, having already failed the first, third, and fifth grades. Yet I still didn't understand why I couldn't learn. No matter how hard I tried, I just couldn't seem to pick up the thread of what was being said. In the midst of this constant struggle, tortured by the sense that there was something drastically wrong with me, I turned to drugs and alcohol to numb the self-doubt and confusion. Eventually, I found myself constantly fantasizing about exotic ways to die—thoughts that were both frightening and oddly comforting when life seemed especially bleak.

"One particularly depressing day, I stood up in the middle of my math class, walked out to my car, and drove straight to the local Army enlistment station. When I got there, I told the officer that I wanted to join the Army and be a helicopter machine gun operator in Vietnam. In the back of my mind, I just figured this would be the best way to end it all and still look like a hero and not just some confused kid who checked out and left his parents to explain. A month later, I left for basic training at Fort Knox, Kentucky. Strangely enough, I really enjoyed it; it was like one big game of sports. After being promoted to private first class, I was sent to Fort Rucker, Alabama, for helicopter mechanic and machine gunner training. Once again, I excelled and by the time it ended I was promoted to corporal and sent not to Vietnam but to Korea where, much to my disappointment, I was put in charge of the motor pool. Gradually, the old patterns began creeping back and before long I was again having serious problems with drugs and alcohol. When I was transferred to Germany in 1970, I began dealing large quantities of drugs—with the 'big boys.' One day in Munich, in the midst of one of the biggest drug deals ever, I had a frightening experience that stopped me in my tracks and made me take a long, hard look at what could happen if I continued on that path. I was driving a rental car with a friend and a stranger from whom we were attempting to buy $10,000 of narcotics. Suddenly, my friend and the stranger began fighting over the gun in the back seat. Thinking I should help, I quickly pulled over to the side of the road and opened the car door. Just as I stepped out, the gun fired directly through my seat—in the exact place where I had been sitting just moments earlier—and, within a few moments, the stranger had vanished with the money *and* the drugs. The fact that I had almost been killed was not a big issue; what shook me was the fact that I could easily have hurt or killed someone else.

"A few days later, when I was sharing the story with a friend of mine who was involved in Alcoholics Anonymous, he stopped me mid-sentence and said, 'You need to come to AA with me. I want you to meet this women named Flobird who has a *real* relationship with God.' For some reason, I listened. When I look back on my life, I can clearly see that this was the point where the angels really started working with me, sending into my life people who showed me an aspect of God and of religion that was very different than anything I had ever been taught. That night, I found myself in a room with about 15 other people—all with a history of drug and alcohol abuse. But the woman who led the group—Flobird, who would eventually become my first spiritual teacher—changed my life.

"From the moment I met her, I felt as if, simply by her presence, she rekindled a desire to know God and truth that I had felt as long as I could remember. As she shared her story, I made a decision to stop the drugs and the alcohol and to turn my life over to God. For the next eight years, the program became my life. Yet, despite the fact that it brought me a great deal of awareness of life, it didn't change my negative thinking habits and I continued to live in a state of pain. Eventually, I realized that if I were going to continue to grow, I would need more information—not a particularly pleasant thought since the image of myself as 'stupid' was quite powerful. A few days later, I heard a voice in my heart say: 'Thomas, you learn what you *want* to learn. Not what people say you *should* learn. What *you* decide to learn.' It marked a major turning point. I realized *I* had the choice and whatever I chose to learn, I could learn; it didn't have to be difficult.

"From that moment forward, I set out on a journey to learn everything I could about God. Eight years later, I moved to Virginia. By then, married with two children, I had left AA. We had made the move so I could enroll in a seminary program with Paul Solomon in the Shenandoah Valley to become a minister in the Fellowship of the Inner Light, an interfaith church with centers around the world. While I was busy with my studies, my wife worked as a nurse at a nearby hospital on the night shift. Every night after she would leave for work and the children were in bed, I would begin to pray and meditate. It was at this time that, quite by accident, I discovered the Angelic Kingdom. Inevitably, when I lay down to meditate, I would experience an overwhelming sense that someone was in the house. Confused and afraid, I would search the entire house, from attic to basement, and each time I would find nothing. Yet, if I resumed my meditation, the feeling of a presence in the house would return. Finally, after much frustration, I asked Paul to come over one night and join me in my meditation. As we began to relax and the strange feeling began again, I asked him if he too felt the presence of someone in the house. To my delight, he said, 'Yes. The visitors are angels. It is time for you to begin to learn how to be sensitive to their presence.' From that moment forward, my work with the angels began to take off. Before long, I was traveling around the world teaching people about the Angelic Kingdom. No one was more surprised than I."

Chapter Two

The Kingdom of Heaven Is at Hand

Dearly Beloved,
It is with great joy that we await your response, for all have been called. Move from the darkness and stand in the light, for there will be but a shadow. Become immersed in the light and there will be the Kingdom of Heaven before you.

The Angels

As we approach the end of a millennium, the cosmic hourglass is spilling its last grains, signaling a pivotal time in history. At this historical moment, as we move from the Age of Pisces to the Age of Aquarius, we are preparing for an evolutionary turning point, the completion of a 26,000-year period of time that marks the end of four yugic cycles. According to Hindu tradition, each *yuga* can be compared to a season in a super-cosmic year. At the end of each yugic cycle, a graduation occurs of all souls that have lived during that cycle of time. Those who have mastered the lessons taught in the Great Mystery School of Earth will progress to another cycle of evolution, and those who do not will come to live again amidst yet another yuga until what is necessary to remember, is remembered.

When the Earth, as we know it, first came into being, it marked the beginning of the *Sathya Yuga* or the Golden Age. During this cycle, humanity lived in a Garden of Eden in harmony with all the other kingdoms, and angels were as naturally accepted as the existence of human beings. As time passed and humankind progressed through the second and third yugic cycles, the *Treta Yuga* or Silver Age and the *Dvapara Yuga* or Copper Age, humankind gradually became more earthbound and distanced from the awareness of a myriad of other life forms and kingdoms and superphysical realities that express life. At present, as we near the completion of the final yugic cycle—the *Kali Yuga* or Iron Age—many have forgotten their divine origins and fear and ignorance are rampant.

But it also marks the dawning of a new cycle of time that will be the culmination of all that has been learned and experienced since our world began—yet another Golden Age, a time the ancients long ago prophesied would be the "the era of the gods' return." As this cyclical "changing of the guard" is collectively experienced, we can expect—and are now experiencing—many dramatic and unprecedented changes as our solar system spirals into a higher orbital frequency, increasing the vibrational speed of Earth and causing an acceleration of energy as never before.

As Light Intensifies, the Illusion of Darkness Is Exposed

But there is more. The yugic cycles are also related to the time it takes for our sun to revolve around a larger sun, termed the Central Sun, the source from which our sun receives its energy. Though its radiance has not yet been measured by our present scientific instruments, according to theosophical teachings this Central Sun is said to be an unseen body of energy that surrounds our sun in much the same fashion as the etheric body surrounds our human body.

With each complete revolution of our sun around this Central Sun, our sun's vibrational frequency—expressed as light—increases. This stepped-up vibrational frequency is then passed down to Earth, causing matter to vibrate at an accelerated rate. Since our physical bodies are composed of matter, this higher vibration of light also steps up the vibrational level of our bodies. As vibrations step up, awareness expands and we begin to perceive life from an entirely new perspective.

As the light penetrates the Earth, it illuminates and "refines" everything unlike it. This spiritualizing effect is experienced, at present, as a healing crisis—a Grand Divine Purification— as what has been termed by masters throughout the ages as the *veil* begins to lift. This veil is composed of all the lies and illusions and erroneous beliefs about life that have literally veiled and distorted our understanding of the meaning and purpose of life since we lived in the Garden of Eden. Throughout the centuries, as more and more of humanity misperceived truth, this veil thickened, clouding our vision of truth and cloaking our consciousness in ignorance.

At this evolutionary turning point when the veil is lifting, the voices of tradition are slowly losing power. Those who continue to experience life on the basis of old belief systems and fixed realities of the past—fear, doubt, confusion—are thrown into turmoil and struggle to maintain control in a world where the old ways no longer work and life appears highly unstable.

Those who are willing to release the past and genuinely commit themselves to creating a different future will experience magic; a changing of perception and consciousness at will, a time when hearts and minds will become aware of a whole new way of living based on unity and oneness and a sense of being a part of one big global family.

The Awakening of Oneness

As we approach the end of the millennium and prepare to usher in yet another Golden Age, what does the future hold for the Earth and its inhabitants?

Are we, as some have said, teetering on the brink of destruction or is it the start of wondrous new age? One thing is clear: change is in the air and, for some, that change may well mean radical transformation.

Flo Calhoun, author of *I Remember Union: The Story of Mary Magdalena*, (All Worlds Publishing, 1992) who channels The Nameless Ones, calls this time the "most monumental pivotal span of consciousness ever, a time to focus on what is clearly coming together, emerging from within, and what is now available for expression—a time to focus on what are called the 'seeds of contentment.'"

According to Calhoun:

> We are moving from the Piscean Age of reason, where the rational, mental, practical and formed are stressed and define reality, to the Aquarian Age, a time of balance where the masculine and feminine, the seen and unseen, and the unknown and, as yet, unformed are acknowledged as equally important. During this time, the feminine essence of nurturance, sustenance and innate order emerges to create a safe and sacred world. In this place of safety, based on intuition and a respect for the sacredness of all life, our potential has its greatest opportunity ever for actualization since the perfect environment will exist where each of us can experience the catalyzing of the potential within, from the "seeds of contentment."

This seed of contentment is our essential self, the essence of who we are and what we've come here to do—the blueprint of our most perfect destiny designed by us and encoded into our being long before we took our first breath here. This seed is literally in the center of our chest, according to Calhoun, in the soul, located under the pointed bone called the xiphoid process.

> Here the seed begins to sprout organically, and the feminine emerges to sustain creativity, inner knowing and sensitivity. An underlying innate process then comes forth which is not directed by the mind—a process so ancient and yet so newly determined from our choice and evolution that it is both predestined and ever-unfolding. With this monumental shift in perspective, this experience of magic, we discover that we belong here and are creating a world with meaning and purpose. As a result, the perfect environment for peace and union is created as the seeds of contentment sprout.

And there is nothing we need to do to experience it. Since it is already within us, we need only recognize it and allow our true selves to unfold. As the seed sprouts and we begin to live our dreams, we bloom into the expression of what we have always dreamed we would become, seeing ourselves fully individual and contributing to the greater whole as we all more fully live our inner seeds of contentment and work together to build an entirely new future.

According to Calhoun, as we move into the 21st century, more and more people will experience this blooming, initiating a quantum leap in consciousness. Even those who were previously unaware of their potential to experience innate contentment will then feel the excitement that is building in and around our planet and join in the wave which is being created. As this contentment emerges, it is upheld by the common vision within and is easily accessed and acted upon. Calhoun explains:

> Then, instead of living in a cause and effect dichotomy where we are taught that we are separate and limitation is a fact, we begin to live the actual experience of unity in a universe that has no boundaries. The inner seed shows us the picture of oneness. The result is a relationship with the greater experience of being that is so profound that we no longer think of loss, or abandonment, survival or how to change the world. All that exists are access points to fulfillment. Then it is no longer frightening to be alive; it is graceful and creative to be alive.

As collectively we bloom, and "gardens" are planted across the globe, we co-create a divine union within and without. And it is not through trying or thinking or striving; it is from a deep inner place of truth which emerges to include us all in the light of oneness, the feminine and masculine sustaining union in form, bringing the inner vision into the outer experience, and co-creating the Kingdom of Heaven here on Earth.

Hear the Angels Sing

At this pivotal moment in our history when divine power is flooding our solar system, co-creating the Kingdom of Heaven on Earth is precisely what the angels have come to help us do.

As the Earth moves into a higher vibrational frequency, raising the vibration of all physical matter and consciousness, our vibrations are gradually becoming closer in frequency to those of the superphysical and invisible realms, and people everywhere are becoming more aware of the invisible angelic hosts that have been guiding and assisting our evolution since the beginning. As we prepare to step across this cyclical threshold, the angels are taking their places and assuming their assignments in the opening of a whole new chapter in our experience of life on Planet Earth. They come to remind us that we are each part of a magnificent plan unfolding in every octave of life. On the deepest level of our being, we have been preparing to be a part of this awakening for nearly 2,000 years. The angels invite us to join in, and they assist us by helping to shift our perceptions and open our awareness to see truth with what they term fourth-dimensional vision—"the seeing from the heart." At present, the majority of humankind is experiencing third-dimensional awareness. In third-dimensional awareness, life is comprehended through the five senses and within the parameters of time and space. We look at life without seeing deeper to the spirit behind it. If, for example, an angel were to appear, we would have to adjust our entire belief system or deny its presence. As we evolve to higher dimensions of awareness, we develop a faculty for seeing beyond the five senses into what is called fourth-dimensional awareness to see and experience the spirit behind the form. In fourth-dimensional awareness, when physical sight is opened to the purpose and meaning of life and the Shining Ones that guide our every action, we *expect* angels to be present.

In fact, one of the most monumental experiences we can ever have is that moment when we realize that luminous beings, invisible to our outer senses, actually exist. How many of us have not secretly wished in our heart-of-hearts that angels might be real? They are, and they have heard our call and come with great joy to assist in our becoming.

The Coming of the Angels

What are angels? Some say they are messengers—the term *angelos* having derived from the Hebrew expression *mal'akh,* translated as "messenger"—great beings of light who bring wisdom and loving thoughts to stimulate our imaginations and offer us a more complete picture of the Divine Plan. Others say they are guides that stand ready to teach us through our Higher Selves. Some call them guardians, claiming they have arrived to protect us and see us safely home. In truth, angels are simply an expression of God's intimacy, reaching out to make as loving a contact as possible. You see, the real essence of an angel defies classification by our human, linear, three-dimensional minds. With bodies said to be composed of ether, the forms in which they appear to us are assumed for the sake of carrying out their earthly missions. Nonetheless, they are as "real" as we are and move about our solar system to carry out whatever assignments they are given by God.

Angels are believed to belong to a different line of evolution than humans. From earliest times, only a small percentage of angels are said to have incarnated as humans and only for the purposes of evolving more rapidly since the human journey—although more difficult—is said to proceed more quickly than that of the Angelic Kingdom. Thus, in a desire for this experience and on assignment from the Source, angels have at times entered our planet to live as humans, though most eventually return to their own kingdom. Whether in human or angelic form, however, they always come as loving companions to lead us home.

In response to our prayers for help, the Angelic Kingdom has been sent to Earth to prepare our hearts and minds to live the experience of oneness and thus usher in a whole new chapter in life on Planet Earth. And in this time of unprecedented change, as the old order of belief in fear makes way for the new order of absolute confidence in love, angels are here to nudge us into remembering that those whose belief in fear is greater than their belief in love are doubting God and believing in the power of darkness. Unfortunately, that belief manifests as what appears to be destruction. And although this apparent destruction has seemingly come crashing down around us, the angels come to remind us that there is no power great enough to destroy life—which is God. And if we can walk with absolute confidence in our hearts, knowing the truth—that Life lives and nothing has the power to destroy God—we can choose love and co-create the Kingdom of Heaven on Earth.

Life As a Great Mystery School

The challenge is this: Earth is the only planet in the solar system that has a highly evolved species, the Human Kingdom, functioning in a low vibrational frequency—hard, dense, physical matter. Thus, in what is sometimes referred to as the Great Mystery School of Earth, matter is the medium of expression—meaning our physical bodies, which are composed of matter, are the vehicles through which we express life. In Mystery School lingo, this is the major initiation: the great "trial by fire" that humankind will experience on Planet Earth. And because it is natural to gradually become attuned to the energies with which one is most often in contact, collectively we have forgotten our divine origins and have mistakenly taken on the belief that matter is the only reality and what is invisible to the five senses—the host of kingdoms and spirits that also inhabit all life—simply do not exist.

But matter was not intended to be experienced as the reality of life; one might see it as *a* reality, but it is not *the* reality. In *Reflections on the Christ* (Findhorn Publications, 1978), David Spangler explains this particular challenge of living life with matter as the medium of expression by comparing humans to the Ents in Tolkien's novel *The Lord of the Rings*. The Ents were actual living beings who looked like trees, although they were not trees; they had come to be shepherds of trees who tended their growth. Unfortunately, some Ents became so attached to their trees that they became "treeish" and eventually you couldn't distinguish an Ent from a tree.

Like the Ents, we have become so identified with our physical selves that we've forgotten who we really are and why we've come here. Unfortunately, when we're caught up in matter, physical things gain inordinant importance. Like the Ents, we identify ourselves with what we have, or what we think, or what we think we are. And since our vehicle of expression is matter and matter will eventually change form, this particular misconception is the cause of much suffering since everything we think we are, and virtually everything we think we have, will experience change and, eventually, apparent destruction.

The point is not to dishonor matter, but simply to recognize that, as the angels say, the Human Kingdom has married matter rather than the Source of matter; and it is the Source of matter that we must honor in all living things. Since all living things that have been created have been created by this Source, He is everywhere present in every creation in countless different variations. Thus, to dismiss matter as "gross" or "illusionary" is to overlook truth.

But in this Great Mystery School of Earth, we have come to learn through experience—since experience is the only means by which humankind can truly learn—all that matter has to teach us. And just as in the actual mystery schools, organizations that have existed throughout history, when prospective students in the Mystery School of Earth reach a certain level of readiness and demonstrate through their expression that they are ready to learn the mysteries behind all life, a teacher will seek them out and begin to instruct through the students' life experiences. In the Earth school, this teacher can appear in virtually any form—for many, the form is now that of an angelic being.

Although angels have been guiding our advancement and responding to our prayers since the beginning, at present they are appearing more frequently because of shifts in our collective consciousness. And not a moment too soon. What's more, because of who and what they are, angels are particularly well-suited to assist us in this current phase of our evolutionary journey.

You see, angels are masters when it comes to shaking our consciousness loose from the illusory belief that matter is all that is real; for the angels, matter is not, nor has it ever been, the medium of their expression. Dwelling constantly in ever-present oneness with God, they express love without limits and fly on the wings of joy, forever coaxing us to join them in taking ourselves lightly. In particular, they have come to help remind earthbound souls of the purpose and meaning of their experience in the Great Mystery School of Earth.

In the words of the well-known clairvoyant Edgar Cayce: "In the beginning, when there was the creating, or the calling of individual entities into being, we were made to be companions with the Father-God." Angels are the intermediaries between kingdoms: the messengers as well as the message, that help us to remember this birthright as companions and co-creators with the Father. Since they are the embodiment of the attributes of the Father-God, they help us see beyond our present so-called reality and remember who we really are. In fact, the true significance of angels is what they express and thus, by their very presence, teach: a constant experience of unity and oneness with God and all living things. If the concept of "oneness" is difficult to comprehend, consider this: for angels, the concept of "I" and the concept of "we" are one and the same. An angel can be itself, or the whole, or, for that matter, literally all things at once. To the angels, it matters not what their assignments may be; to serve is their greatest joy.

Amidst the dense vibrations of matter, we tend to forget this experience of oneness and instead experience ourselves as separate and alone—set adrift in a dangerous world where we are forced to survive. Angels have come to show us a new way, a way of living life in harmony with Universal Laws of Cause and Effect, what the angels have suggested we call Universal Agreements.

Universal Agreements are simple, immutable laws—endless in number—by which all life operates. Created by God in harmony with a universal code of unconditional love, they are written on our hearts and, when applied, give rise to all that is good in life. Universal Agreements are different from what is termed "reality." Since creation began they have always existed. What we term reality is something else: what the majority agrees on at any particular moment in history, subject to change from one generation to the next. Universal Agreements do not change; and when we resist or violate them, the natural harmony of life is prevented and the next step in the evolution of all life, which is dependent upon this harmony, is delayed.

But Planet Earth is a planet where humankind is given free will and full responsibility for how we exercise our choices. This faculty of free will determines our attitudes and beliefs and the sum total of our experiences. With this capacity for free will choice, we can collectively choose to remember these Universal Agreements written on our hearts, or choose not to remember them. In short, we can choose heaven or we can choose hell. The angels have arrived to assist us in remembering and to show us that, when we live in harmony with these agreements, pain and suffering will no longer be a part of our experience.

For instance, what is called the Universal Agreement of Correspondence maintains that everything in life is interdependent and part of the whole—in short, that we are one Divine Family. Thus, anything that is not in harmony with this Universal Agreement such as separation, competition, or even selfishness, leads to imbalance, disharmony and inevitably discord and suffering. By their very presence and nature, the angels demonstrate this agreement and nudge us to remember that, as we live in harmony with the agreement, we fulfill the evolutionary design.

Yet another of the most basic agreements is the Universal

Agreement of Karma that suggests that "what goes around comes around" and each time it does, it is an opportunity to find balance. When we react to life, we recreate the same emotional, mental, and physical patterns we are reacting to and fail to notice the opportunity available to change; we extend our karma and continue to meet similar lessons again and again. When we respond to life with love, we fulfill the Universal Agreement of Karma by changing our patterns, choosing new options, and experiencing gratitude. Then we experience grace—the experience of God, or love, operating in all of life.

The angels have come to offer an entirely new perspective on karma; although it has been defined as punishment and retribution, a painful "wheel" careening out of control, in actuality karma is a blessing from God, an opportunity to transform the lesson and change the experience—once and for all. Karma is God's way of saying, "No matter how many times you react, I will constantly make the way available and await your return to Me." When we call on the angels for assistance, they teach us—by their loving presence that accepts us for what we truly are—to live in harmony with the Universal Agreement of Karma; to respond with love to everything in life. When we live in harmony with the Universal Agreement of Karma, collectively we will begin to see the beauty and magnificence of Earth, rather than the suffering and chaos—and this simple agreement fulfilled becomes the key to living in the Kingdom of Heaven while here on Earth.

According to the angels, all these Universal Agreements that are written on our hearts are the guideposts that will show us the steps we need to take so that life can be lived with more meaning and joy. The required steps are not restrictive; in fact, the purpose of the Universal Agreements is to manifest the infinite love of the Source. Edgar Cayce said, "To spirit, to spirits, Universal Law must all come. The nearer we apply those laws in keeping with divine love, the greater the blessings to self and the greater the blessing of self upon others." When we call on the angels and invite them into our lives as teachers, guides, friends, and loving companions, they awaken our remembrance of the Universal Agreements; when we apply them, we experience a New Heaven and a New Earth.

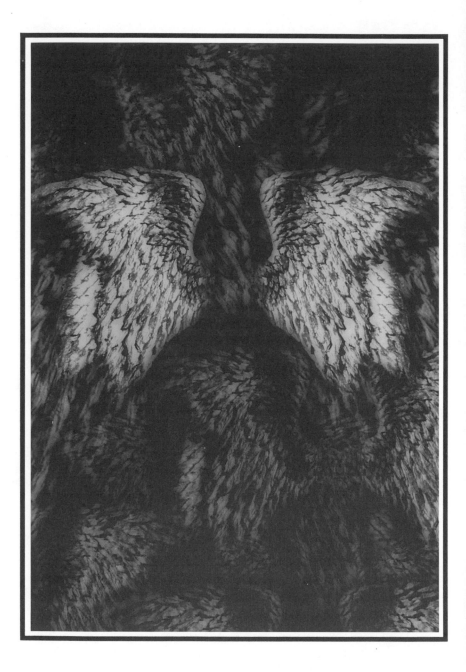

Chapter Three

The Great Symphony of Life:
A Creation Story From the Angels

Dearly Beloved,
Let us be clear. There is but One God, One Source, One
Father of all. This one Source of life is the holy I AM. This
One Source lives and moves and has its Being in and around
you. This One Source is best named through the word and
vibration of Love. To know and experience this one Source
is the common goal of all peoples and all life. To experience
this One Source is to express the love that you are. It is that
simple. Express and experience this love in your work and
in your play and you will come face to face with your Source.
The Angels

We would at this time wish to tell you a story, a story that we will direct to your heart that you might best understand what many have called the Triad Heavens or The Hierarchy of Order of the Angelic Kingdoms. And what many have referred to as the hierarchy, or order of authority or power, we would call an *assignment* for it is neither authority nor power that the consciousness of Oneness would design, for when life was manifested, everything—even the Human Kingdom—was not a "creation" of God, but God Himself manifesting in form. Thus, every manifestation "made in the image and likeness of God" is separate from that which we will call the Great Absolute, but, in truth, one and the same.

We are calling this a story for the heart to demonstrate that you can experience God most effectively from the feeling level as you allow the heart to speak to that part of the mind that can dream dreams and imagine itself into the realm of spirit; you see, Dearly Beloved, learning does not come through words or information. Experience is the way of learning for the Human Kingdom and the builder of wisdom for those who choose truth.

So, quiet your mind and open your heart and we will tell you the story we will call the Great Symphony of Life.

The Great Symphony of Life

Long, long ago, before time was, lived the Great Absolute. And this Great Absolute was all love, all peace, and all that has ever been and all that will ever be and there was nothing that He was not. And it came to pass that this Most High God, steeped in love and light and alive with limitless potential, decided in His infinite wisdom to express and manifest His eternal nature in the form of a great celestial symphony in order that He might share His unbounded love and continue to expand everlasting.

And so it was that from where the Divine Musician rested in absolute equilibrium there began at that moment to sound forth the mighty creative chords and this Great Sound, the Great Audible Logos, caused that which was beyond manifestation to begin to move, that which was vibrationless to extend into life as vibration. And as this Sound began to cause Creation everywhere, all worlds and all kingdoms began to come into existence. And as this great outpouring of sound permeated the whole entire universe, love was the substance and love the foundation, constantly radiating out in the form of vibration to create all life and the heavens and the planets; and everything was filled with Himself and nothing existed without being in Him because He was everywhere present and in everything alive He did live.

The First Angels of the First Triad Heaven
The Holy Seraphim

As this great symphony sounded forth, there manifested the First Heavens and what are known as the Holy Seraphim, each with six wings to cover his face and his feet and to fly. "Above it stood the Seraphim: each one had six wings; with twain he covered his face, and with twain he covered his feet, and with twain he did fly." (Isaiah 6:2)

And as these winged ones sang forth the song of creation, gathering the vibrations emanating from God and sending them out into space, they assumed their assignment as lords of the Higher Mind to guard all visions and ideals of love and lift all consciousness toward all six dimensions that all might be reborn in the Light.

And as they chanted their eternal praise—*Holy, Holy, Holy is the name of God; Holy, Holy, Holy is the lord of the Host*—the Seraphim became the great sounding force of life heard and felt through the hearts of all living things as Pure Thought, Pure Light, Pure Love, and with these attributes as building blocks and from the vibration of their chants, the worlds began to form.

The Second Angel in the First Triad Heaven
Cherubim

And as this great everlasting expansion continued to sound forth, there manifested the second angel of the First Triad Heaven, the Cherubim, each with four wings and four faces and each with the face of a man and an ox and a lion and an eagle. And as they moved through the heavens, they assumed their assignment to allow life to see from the perspective of each of the directions so that each would experience the fullness of the Great Absolute in all life and all living things.

And as they emanated the wisdom and awareness of all that God is, the Cherubim became the holy guardians to guard ideals and forms, rituals, and places, that life would be protected from all discord.

The Third Angel in the First Triad Heaven
Thrones—Ophanim—Wheels

And there sounded forth the third angel in the First Triad Heaven, the Thrones, each with thousands of eyes and appearing like a wheel inside a wheel. And in a gesture of love, they assumed their assignment to manifest God in the form of matter, radiating out their constancy and steadfastness, stabilizing the whole created universe from that place where heaven and earth are together as One.

The First Angels of the Second Triad Heaven
Dominions

And there sounded forth the first angel of the Second Triad Heaven, the holy Dominions, who assumed their assignment to regulate the duties of the angels and those of the created universe to make certain all was in accordance with God's Divine Plan. And as they played forth their music to allow the majesty and mercy of the Great Absolute to manifest in form, making certain all life was good, they expressed the attributes of order and kindness for all life and all living things.

The Second Angel of the Second Triad Heaven
Virtues

And there sounded forth the second angel of the Second Triad Heaven, the Virtues, who assumed their assignment to become the heavenly guardians to guide and protect all living attributes of the one Great Absolute. And as they began to bestow blessings from on high, they brought forth grace and miracles that all life would experience truth.

The Third Angel of the Second Triad Heaven
Powers

And there sounded forth the third angel of the Second Triad

Heaven, the Powers, who assumed their assignment to police the heavens and Earth, bringing order and harmony through the balancing of duality and the expression of justice and mercy for all living things.

The First Angel of the Third Triad Heaven
Principalities

And there sounded forth the first angel of the Third Triad Heaven, the Principalities, who assumed their musical assignment to preside over and protect the religions and leaders of Earth, inspiring and directing nations, provinces, and rulers so the Divine Plan would be fulfilled and all would experience unity with the Great Absolute and all His manifestations throughout the universe.

The Second Angel of the Third Triad Heaven
The Holy Archangels

And there sounded forth the second group of angels of the Third Triad Heaven, the Holy Archangels who sang their musical assignment from each of the four directions, purifying and uplifting and ministering to the legions of angels and all life and all living things.

The most well-known, from each of the four directions, we will share with you here.

And there sounded forth Archangel Michael from the East, Chief of Archangels and Prince of Light, who sang forth his assignment as the embodiment of the Great Symphony, and the Watcher of Souls who, in love and concern for all living things, stood ready to guide all souls to awaken and follow the path of love to return to the Great Absolute.

And there sounded forth Archangel Raphael from the South, Regent of the Sun and Chief of the Order of Virtues, who sang forth his assignment as the great healer of Earth whose vitality and mercy would bring the transformative fire of passion and love to guard creative talent and science and knowledge and to heal all life and all living things.

And there sounded forth Archangel Uriel from the West, Face of God and Angel of Prophecy, who sang forth his assignment as the force of thought and to express determination and action to inspire and convey holy ideas to writers and teachers and reveal the glory of earth.

And there sounded forth Archangel Gabriel from the North, Archangel of Good News and Interpreter of Dreams, who sang forth her musical assignment to manifest Truth with icy clarity as the force of nourishment and cleansing so that all life would know all are One.

The Third Angel of the Third Triad Heaven
The Holy Ones or Angels

And there sounded forth the third group of angels from the Third Triad Heavens, The Holy Ones, the youngest of angels who, under the tutelage of other angelic hierarchies, assumed their assignment to serve humankind and fulfill the Divine Plan through expression of the attributes of the Great Absolute.

HUMAN KINGDOM

And as the Great Symphony sounded forth, there manifested the Human Kingdom, who assumed their assignment to become the Crowning Glory of the Earth experience made in the image and likeness of God. And as they played forth their music, they became companions to the Great Absolute with the holy assignment of co-creating the Kingdom of Heaven on Earth.

THE EARTH KINGDOMS

And as the Great Symphony sounded forth, there manifested the Elementals, or spirits of the elements, called by some the Brownies, Pixies, or Gnomes, who sang forth their holy assignment to express and experience the attributes of God, in what might be called the building blocks of matter in the veins of stones and mineral within and throughout the Earth; and the

Sylphs, or spirits of the air, who sang forth their assignment to express and experience the attributes of God in and through the air; and the Sprites or Undines, spirits of water, who sang forth their assignment to express and experience the attributes of God in and through water on Earth as well as water within the human body; and the Salamanders, spirits of fire, who sang forth their assignment to express and experience the attributes of God in and through fire.

PLANT KINGDOM

And as the Great Symphony sounded forth, there manifested the Devas, who sang forth their holy assignment to govern and lord over the life force in the plants and vegetables and flowers and trees.

THE ANIMAL KINGDOM

As the Great Symphony sounded forth, there manifested the Aqui, called the Budiels or Folatels, who sang forth their holy assignment as oversoul guardians to animals to watch over the evolution of the species and care for their physical needs.

And so it was and so it is, all a great symphony ever being composed and performed as the everlasting Music of the Spheres.

A note about Dark or Fallen Angels: The story of these angels are either allegories or metaphors to assist the Human Kingdom in understanding what can happen if you believe you are not one with God and all life and all living things. Life, and that which lives, cannot be separate from God, for if that were to happen, in that moment of separation that expression of life would no longer exist. In truth, this idea of separation from Source has not ever been experienced, for God cannot abandon a part of Himself.

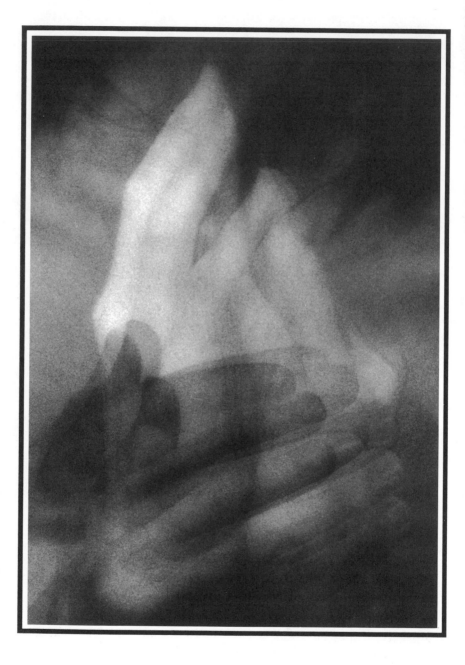

Chapter Four

Prayer, Meditation and Faith: Opening the Door To the Angelic Kingdoms

Dearly Beloved,
We invite you to open your hearts and minds to the
Father, that we might introduce to you the glory and peace
that comes with the immense creative energies which are
now about you. There are two agreements which will make
this more abundant for you. First, we ask that you open your
hearts that you might find the ability to channel God's Love.
Secondly, we would ask you to focus your minds and hearts
in the experience of the Now for it is only in the now that
one can know the love and essence of God. The moment
where you are is the moment of knowing.
The Angels

Many people have asked us why they can't see the angels, or why they can't hear them—and of course, how they can. The important point to keep in mind is that angels come into our awareness in whatever form we will allow them, but it is often in ways that seem somewhat alien to our usual forms of listening and communicating. They do not come bearing megaphones. You have to allow yourself an opportunity for quiet time, time to reflect on your life and time to listen for their particular brand of celestial assistance.

Some people hear the angels, some people simply sense their presence. Other people see them in the form of lights, or in that of a beautiful human-like creature; still others experience them as a mysterious urge to do something, distinctly out of character, that turns out to be the perfect action to have taken at that particular moment. Some simply sense them as a sudden flash of insight. Thomas, for example, doesn't see them; he senses their presence and suddenly receives from the angels concepts and ideas that are often very different than his usual way of perceiving life. Suddenly, he'll feel lighter, and situations that once seemed impossible become clear with new meaning and purpose. My most common experience is one of seeing them in the form of spontaneous visions that unfold in my mind, much like waking dreams.

One particularly challenging day, for example, during the writing of this book when it seemed as if the events of my life were conspiring to keep me from completing it, I suddenly saw a vision while driving down a crowded highway. In my mind's eye, I saw myself riding what seemed to be a powerful stallion that spooked, reared up, and was about to throw me to the ground. As I struggled to somehow pull in the reins, a voice said, "Let go." When I did, the stallion calmed down and began to calmly graze with me still perched on his back. In an instant, I got the message. I realized that if I didn't relax and accept the guidance coming from the angels rather than feeling I had to do it by myself, I would stop the flow, "rein in" my creativity and stop any angelic input in the process. Clearly, it was time to let go and let the angels assist. As if in confirmation of the vision, when I later met a client for lunch, as I explained the chaotic and complicated events of my life, she smiled sweetly and said, "Guess it's time to let go and let God."

Coincidence? Synchronicity? Or the influence of angels. For me, the fact that the momentary vision helped me to see beyond the almost unbearable frustration and entertain another perspective was proof enough that divine assistance was the culprit in this particular case.

But visions aren't the only way in which the angels can appear. They can also appear in messages garnered from our surroundings. This is, in fact, another way the angels often make themselves available in my life, as well as in Thomas's. When we first conceived of the book—and I was feeling more than unequal to the task—I was alone on my daily trek through the woods when I found myself wondering how I could possibly define an angel. Suddenly, I was startled out of my reverie when my attention shifted and my eyes were strangely drawn up above the trees. Without knowing why, I became engrossed in staring up at an uncommonly beautiful sky. A flawless robin's-egg blue and cloudless, it was more beautiful than anything I could remember seeing. And when I looked down at the lake in the distance, I suddenly realized that I could see in the water below an exact reflection of the blue of the sky and a perfect reproduction of every limb on every tree. In an instant (this is also how I know it was an superphysical communication—my mind doesn't work that quickly) I experienced a deep sense of knowing that the calm surface of the lake and the angels are actually very similar. Angels, too, are like mirrors; when we allow ourselves to experience them, what we experience is a reflection of our true divine nature.

Angel Assistance Can Change Your Mind

Angels are masters at assisting us with subtle perspective shifts such as the one I experienced at the lake. When we respond to this particular variety of angelic assistance and see life from a higher perspective, we often discover we've suddenly changed our minds. And since, in the words of Edgar Cayce, "mind is the builder" of our experience, changing our minds is a powerful first step. When our thoughts are no longer limited by our mindset, neither is our expression limited, or our experience; in short, we can literally change our entire experience of life by changing our minds. The challenge is to get quiet enough to hear what the angels are trying to convey; if you call on them, even if you call on the great Archangels, they *will* respond within twenty-four hours. There is no choice—that is their assignment from the Father, and, in the Angelic Kingdom, the angels do not experience free will. They express whatever attribute of God they have been assigned to express—and always with joy.

It is important to understand that angelic assistance is available to everyone—in fact, it's our very birthright to co-create our dreams with God and the celestial beings that have come to guide and teach us. And we don't have to earn this right, and we certainly don't have to be more holy. To the angels, the Human Kingdom has never been anything but holy; it's simply a matter of belief. However, there are certain age-old techniques that can help us become more receptive to hearing and sensing more subtle dimensions: relaxation, prayer, meditation, and faith—and always with an open heart. When our hearts are open and receptive, we remember that each of us is searching for an experience of intimacy with the Source of all life, and that Source is Love. For many of us, the mind has not yet accepted this concept.

Relaxing Into More Subtle Dimensions

When you're stressed, blood flow is restricted, oxygen is restricted, and life force energy moving through your body is restricted. Consider the analogy of a barometer: if it measures from 1 to 10, with relaxation as 1 and ultimate tension as 10, each step up the barometer causes a deadening and numbing of the physical body, as well as the heart, mind, and awareness. By the time the barometer reads 10, you are so rigid that it actually hurts when someone touches you. Yet a person who is 100-percent relaxed can work with the life energy in and around them and open to dimensions beyond the five senses. As sensitivity is enhanced, it becomes easier to access these more subtle dimensions and infinitely easier to hear the angels—and the universe—sing.

One of the things you may notice is that, as you relax, your heart begins to open. You begin to experience a lack of tension and a sense of well-being. It is easy to lose this sense of ease over the years and gradually become more fearful and guarded. Yet if, even for an instant, you were to drop your fears and remember that feeling you had as a child when life seemed perfect just as it was, you could view your life and those around you from a wonderfully different perspective than your normal vantage point. And, when you do, you may notice the host of heavenly angels nurturing you forward to fulfill your wildest dreams.

A Relaxation Exercise From the Angels

It is suggested by the Angels that you might use a tape recorder to record the exercises and invocations in this book. The tapes will allow you to relax more completely into each exercise and invocation, as well as experience it more fully. They will also give you an opportunity to utilize the exercises whenever and wherever you wish.

> *Dearly Beloved,*
> *When you are tending to learn and become familiar with the spirit that is behind all life, as well as the different kingdoms, you will want to learn to relax into the awareness and the experience of these more subtle energies. Thus relaxation becomes perhaps the most valuable point to consider in communication with the various kingdoms and spirit of life. It's important to recognize that most humans are not aware of how stressed they are in any given moment or, for that matter, how to experience relaxation. So, to begin, consciously decide to become more relaxed and throughout the day repeat often, "I can always let go a little more." Gradually you will then teach yourself to experience and express life from a state of awareness, a state of consciousness, and a state of responsiveness that is also a state of relaxation.*

Conscious Breathing

Breathing is an extremely important key in relaxation and effective living. As you breathe, you obviously breathe in life itself, filling the body with oxygen and the essence of life. What's more, if breathing is shallow, you will usually think in shallow terms; when you breathe deeply, you think with more depth and awareness.

Just for a moment, stop and close your eyes and become aware of your breathing. Don't try to manipulate your breathing; try not to pick up pace, or slow down, or breathe more deeply, or breathe in a more shallow fashion. Simply become aware of your normal pattern of breathing. Do you breathe with slow, deep breaths, or short, fast, or shallow breaths? Get a sense of your normal breathing pattern. Watch your breath. One of the things you'll begin to notice is that if you stop and focus, as soon as you focus on your breath, you automatically start to become a little more relaxed. Most of you will find it necessary to practice your breathing, learning to breathe with a normal rhythm, slowly filling the lungs from the bottom all the way up to the top of the shoulders, breathing in through the nose and out through the mouth. What you will begin to notice is that there is a difference in how you feel when you breathe in through the nose and out through the mouth. Allow yourself to be sensitive and watch your body's response to these experiences.

As to the physical position for your relaxation exercise, technically you can do your meditations standing up, sitting, or even lying down. For most people, it is a matter of experimentation to find which position and which exercises work best for you. Some of you will find lying down is best, while some will go to sleep if you lie down. The traditional posture is to sit in a chair with the spine erect, holding the head straight, and, in most instances, with the feet planted firmly on the floor and the hands resting in your lap.

Regulating Your Breath

The first series of exercises is to assist you in regulating your breathing pattern and bring it into harmony with some of the other rhythms already in the body. You can do this in a couple of ways. First, with two of your fingers from either hand, find a place on your body where you can very comfortably monitor the rhythm of your heartbeat. (You can easily find a pulse on the jugular vein that runs along either side of the neck.) Now, breathe in through the nose and count as you inhale, using the rhythm of your heartbeat, filling your lungs from the bottom to the top, slowly breathing in the breath of life. You might want to see that which you breathe as light, warmth, love, joy, and peace. As you fill the lungs from bottom to top, begin to count eight pulses: one, two, three, four, five, six, seven, eight. At the count of eight, stop your inhale and retain the breath for four counts of your pulse. Begin to exhale through the mouth now for eight counts of your pulse. On the exhale there is no holding of the breath; you will breathe in through the nose for the count of eight pulses, hold for the count of four pulses, then exhale through the mouth for eight pulses. On the next pulse, begin your inhale again, doing this also eight complete cycles. As you do, see your inhale as the breathing in of God's love, peace, and joy. Holding this peace on your exhale, see all stress and tension be exhaled out the mouth.

Another exercise you can do is the following. Again, either sit in a comfortable position or lie down; breathe in, filling the lungs from the bottom to the top, and on the inhale through the nose, repeat the affirmation, "I rest in God's love." When the lungs are full, begin your exhale with the affirmation, "I am relaxed." All exercises will work best if done for a twenty-minute cycle as it can take this amount of time to let go of all the activities that go on through the senses and the different levels of consciousness and awareness, and to come to a place of balance and focus. Keep in mind, however, that even at the office or wherever you may be, both of these exercises can be done discreetly. You can do them at your desk, or you can even do them in the restroom for two or three minutes. The eight-count breathing is done for a cycle of eight. The "I rest in God's Love" breathing is done for twenty minutes if possible or, if not, five to ten.

Your Personal Relaxation **OM**

This next exercise requires a little introduction. Consider first the fact that we live in a universe where sound is the cause of creation, a universe where the unmanifested, or that which is vibrationless, manifests as sound. As a result, there is vibration that is set in motion. Therefore, everything that is a manifestation of the Great Symphony of Life is Source manifesting at a specific personal vibration. In this particular exercise, you are going to be experiencing your vibration with the inner ear.

We're going to use this particular exercise because one of the experiences you are learning in working with your angels is how to become more sensitive to the still, small voice within. So you will use this exercise to allow yourself to become aware of and familiar with your personal voice within; what your voice sounds like as well as from whence it comes. To begin, you may want to lie flat on the floor on your back or, if you prefer, on a bed or couch, so there will be less need to control the position of the physical body. However, this exercise can be done sitting as well.

To begin to get into harmony with your vibration, place your thumbs in your ears, closing out any sound from the environment around you. At the same time, place the next two fingers over your closed eyelids. At first, you may notice sounds which remind you of the ocean—perhaps a roaring sound. If you listen very carefully, you will notice there is also an overtone. This is the sound you are listening for. As you place your focus on this overtone, you will begin to hear still another overtone which is a little higher tone. As you begin to hear each higher tone, place your focus on the next highest tone you can hear in any moment, each time moving to the highest tone. When you are hearing the highest tone, you have found your personal true vibration, or your mantra or your personal *OM* vibration. You will discover as you tune into your personal *OM* and sound vibration that this exercise starts to produce automatic relaxation in the body. In fact, you may discover that it feels as though you may have stopped breathing as the breath becomes shallow and the body becomes extremely relaxed and thus begins to respond to its personal vibration.

This exercise can be done as long as time will allow in the moment. This is a perfect exercise to start your day in your morning meditations, as well as a way to end the day before sleep.

The Truth About Prayer

When you are relaxed, you are better able to see the Big Picture. It is from this point of clarity that it is most effective to pray. Why? Because when you're relaxed, your mind is clear, and when your mind is clear, you will ask for what you really want. Simply put, prayer is a "talking to" and because you are always "talking to" someone, either to yourself—running memories of the past through the mind, considering possible futures, or having conversations with the various parts of your psyche—or to someone outside yourself, you are always praying. The question is: to *whom* and to *what* are you praying?

Since prayer is an essential building block of co-creation with the Father, the angels want to help us understand that life is a prayer and assist us in directing our prayers to the highest. Whether you call this the Father, Father/Mother/God, Creator, Universal Self, or Creative Principal, it matters not; only that you direct your "talk" to the highest. And when praying to the Father, just as when communicating with the Angelic Kingdom, the most effective prayers arise from the heart. Though we may sometimes feel silly asking our Source for something when He probably already knows what we want, the asking is more for us than for Him. It re-establishes a companionship relationship and allows us to establish the source of the answer. It also allows us to get clear on exactly what we're asking for; a wise choice since when we ask, we *will* receive an answer.

Remember: prayer does not have to be reverent and we do not have to use certain words or be in a certain rarified state before our prayers are allowed entrance to the holy place to which prayers are delivered. The most effective prayer is a simple, honest conversation with the Father. Simply ask Him to come fully into your life and be a part of everything you do, and ask that He send His angels to assist you.

In the process of writing this book, the angels showed us an entirely new perspective on prayer since, when we wrestled with the fears and doubts about our ability to complete it on time—not to mention the fact that a thousand other demands were often vying for our attention—eventually prayer became the only answer. Many times, when it seemed as if we couldn't go one more step—when, in spite of our efforts, the information needed was simply unavailable—out of the blue the angels would arrive and the information would once again flow, leaving us only the challenge of writing fast enough to get it all! But one thing became strikingly clear: the only possible way to follow through without the frantic feeling that halted any semblance of inspiration was to ask for help. Simply put, prayer was the lifeline—and what we discovered is *that's precisely what prayer is.*

The original Sanskrit word for *prayer* is *pal-al,* meaning "judging oneself as wondrously made." This particular definition suggests how prayer was originally intended. In our prayers, we have an opportunity to experience ourselves as sons and daughters of the Most High, who know without question that it is the Father's good pleasure to give us the Kingdom. And when we pray from that place of absolute clarity about who we are and what it is we want, with heartfelt desire and give ourselves permission to experience fulfillment, we will experience "miraculous" results. In fact, this is among the most important keys to effective prayer. The focused intent concerning what we wish to accomplish and the sincere calling out from the heart that knows no other option for receiving assistance brings results.

Angels are the bridge; they assist us in directing our prayers to the Father and act as messengers to deliver the responses from the Throne of Grace. And though they appreciate our acknowledgement and recognition, they are not interested in being the recipient of our prayers or our worship; that is reserved for the Father, though they may well be the messengers who deliver our requests.

It is also important to recognize that thoughts about ourselves directly affect our prayers. What, for example, do you think happens when you ask a God you have never met and hardly know to give you something you don't believe you actually deserve? Or when you attempt to bargain with God, saying "If I can have this, I will do that." Both arise from a feeling of unworthiness. What's more, there is a difference between praying and begging or pleading. Begging or pleading implies that we don't deserve what we are asking. And when, for example, we don't believe that we deserve to have joy or abundance, it produces confusion and fear that our prayers won't be heard, much less answered. Then, in fact, our lack of belief that we would ever be allowed to experience abundance or joy—since we have free will—becomes what we are praying to; since we believe in lack or pain, we are simply calling it in with our limited imagination and subtly choosing it with our free will. The truth is, we are perfect and loved just as we are and we don't need to petition for something that is already ours; we simply need to reach out our hands. But because we have free will, and we choose to live under the law of Cause and Effect—which says that what we create, we meet, to teach us that we are the Creator—we can't receive what we don't believe we deserve to receive. On the other hand, if we remember who we really are—The Crowning Glory, made in the "image and likeness of God"—virtually anything is possible.

The Power of Prayer

One of the most effective prayers the angels suggested to us is an ancient one that has been with us for centuries. When said with honesty and clear purpose from the heart, it is a very powerful experience.

> Search me O God, and know my heart.
> Wash me, and I shall be clean.
> Purge me with hyssop, and I shall be whiter than snow.
> Make me ready to approach Thy Altar, and to enter Thy
>   Holy Presence.

This particular prayer or atonement is one that we use every time we pray or every time we meditate. With this prayer, we communicate to the highest Source, and ask that He know our hearts, know the true motive of our hearts, and cleanse that motive in love. In spite of all the conflicting thoughts or beliefs that we may have at any given time, this prayer allows us to call our focus to the heart—for in the heart is that "seed of contentment" and that point of balance where we can know that we are "the child in whom God is well-pleased."

As the angels explained in Chapter Four, prayer is a very important component in all that we do in our lives. It continues on a constant basis because prayer is a "talking to." Thus, every thought is a prayer, and therefore one would do well to shepherd, to watch closely, their thoughts since, as each thought goes out, it is a petition to something. When we are not clear, we can put out hundreds of little negative prayers during a day. Then we wonder why things are the way they are. So prayer becomes very important, and the angels suggest that we look carefully at our thoughts and turn them intentionally into prayers so there is nothing that we are unconsciously praying for in our lives. Ask the Source and the angels to help you and assist you through prayer with anything and everything that you may find yourself doing. There's no situation too large, and certainly none too small. If you're not as happy as you might wish to be, for example, pray to your Source and the Angelic Kingdom to respond and call to yourself more happiness, more joy, or more contentment in your life or a specific situation. You can pray for assistance with your job or your family or assistance with abundance and prosperity. Actually, the possibilities are unlimited. Remember, prayers can't be wasted because sound is vibration. So one of the things to keep in mind is that you may want to pray aloud as often as possible because by speaking your prayers aloud you are sending those vibrations out into the universe, and they will reach that to which you have directed them; this is a given. It is the way the universe was made and so it is. For example, if you are praying for peace on Earth, you are contributing to a very positive manifestation of peace for the Earth on a daily basis. It's very important to know with confidence that your prayers of peace are in fact making a difference; whether you can see the difference at any given moment is not the point.

Thomas shares an experience that he had with prayer and the angels just a week before we started this book:

"At the time, we were having problems with our prosperity at the church where I am pastor. So one morning I came into the sanctuary, and I did some breathing exercises to allow myself to get focused. Then I began to communicate to the Father that I wanted help and support with the money situation.

"This is the Prayer:

Heavenly Father, Divine Mother,
In this moment of atonement, I ask that you would come fully into this experience of prayer with me. Become fully a part of all that I may think or do this day. I ask in the nature of Love that all of my life and all of this Center be put under the jurisdiction of our Divine Source. All that is done here, be done in accordance with the will of the highest, with the Source of Life, light, love, joy, and wisdom. Now Father, in this moment of attunement and prayer, touch my mind and my heart, that I might be sensitive to the presence here in this sanctuary of Living Love. And that I might know this presence of Love that lives within me as well.

Now, Father, in this moment of atonement, I would ask that the Center's prosperity and abundance and finances be in harmony, that the Center's income exceed its expenses, and that the funds be available today that this Center may maintain and keep its responsibilities and commitments, and all that we have agreed to respond to. I ask all of this knowing that this Center has a right to the Divine abundance of this universe. This Center now releases any lack or belief in lack, and claims its abundance from its Divine Source. Claiming its abundance in the name of The Father, and of the Son, and of the Holy Spirit. And so it is, and so it shall be. Amen.

"Having finished this prayer, I went about the day. But as the day went on, I have to admit that it was difficult since I continued to be concerned about the situation, despite my prayer. Yet, in my concern, the angels showed me how this is an important point for so many of us: we ask our Source to provide something, and then we forget to trust and let go, to

59

allow the Source to provide. We have a tendency to manipulate people, places, and things, saying, 'Okay, Source, now it can come from here or it can come from there, or we can get it from this person or this situation.' So I spent the day checking the mail, thinking surely this is how God is going to give us what we need. As this day went on, the mail came and there was no money. Yet, I was beginning to feel more secure in the prayer because the angels kept saying all day, 'Decide that if you ask, it will be so.' As the day came to a close, I went to bed that night thanking God and the angels for the day.

"The next morning, as I repeated my routine of meditating in front of the alter in the sanctuary, a most fascinating experience happened. Again, in my meditation and prayer, I was asking that Source take jurisdiction over all that might go on this day, when the money situation popped back into my mind. I began to ask again that the money be made available to pay certain bills and so forth when I very clearly felt and then heard an angel respond very directly: 'Dearly Beloved, you asked for this yesterday. If you truly have faith and confidence in your Source that your prayers are heard and answered, that your Father knows your needs, then the most appropriate thing to do now is not to ask, but simply say to the Father, thank you. Thank your Source for responding to your prayers, for responding to your needs and the Center's needs.'

"So I followed the angel's advice, saying, 'Heavenly Father, thank you for hearing my prayers and responding to the prayer for prosperity.' I then let it go and went about my work for the day. That afternoon a check came for the Center for $1000.00. In the envelope was a card and on the front of the card were the words, 'I was thinking of all the wonderful things God created.' When I opened the card, I read, 'and you and the Fellowship Center came to mind.' But it was the other item in the card that touched me the most. Inside was a rainbow-colored badge which read, 'God keeps His promises.'"

When we state our prayers very clearly and we say to our Source, "This is what I'm asking for, and if it be in my best interest, then please respond to this request," and then thank our Source with an absolute faith and knowing that our prayer has been received and heard, our faith will build that which we are looking for. Faith is the substance; then you simply watch for the divine response, sealing the prayer with a thank-you, knowing that it is being handled in perfect divine order and in perfect timing.

There is an endless number of things that we can ask for in prayer. The key is clarity and confidence. Know what it is you're asking for, ask, and then seal it with a thank-you that says, "I know that I can live my life from this moment on as if this prayer has been heard, and is already being answered."

The more personal and intimate our prayers become, the more powerful and experiential they become as well.

Now it came to pass, As He was Praying in a certain place, when He ceased, one of His disciples said unto Him, "Lord, teach us to pray, as John also taught his disciples." And He said unto them, "When You Pray, say. . ." (Luke 11:1-2)

The Gospel's words *in a certain place* show us that Jesus was in a Certain Place in Himself. When He prayed, His consciousness was in His Heart of Hearts. There He would have a personal experiential conversation with His Father, always personal and intimate.

Understanding With the Angels
the Power of The Lord's Prayer

Our Father which art in heaven, hallowed be thy name. Thy kingdom come, thy will be done in Earth as it is in heaven. Give us this day our daily bread and forgive us our trespasses as we forgive those who trespass against us. And leave us not in temptation but deliver us from evil, for thine is the kingdom, the power, the glory forever and ever. Amen.

Dearly Beloved,
Let us take you on a journey through the words of a great

teacher and see if we can capture and claim the meaning, purpose, and power of what was being shared at the time this was given to humanity.

If we look closely at what has been given here we find that not only is this a prayer, but it also can be appreciated as a formula for how to pray. You will want to keep in mind that the question posed to the Master was not that He would give the apostle a prayer, but that He would "Teach us to pray."

Our Father which art in Heaven. *This formula for prayer starts with two important statements. First, you will notice that "Our" is plural. Thus, you are saying to your Source that there are many parts which make up your beingness. This is the acknowledgement from self to God that you know that the Father is the Source of all aspects of yourself: your mental, physical, emotional, spiritual, etheric, and astral bodies and more. I am addressing this prayer to the Source of all of me. The phrase "which art in Heaven" states where this Father lives, thus recognizing that I know that You live in Heaven, so I send my prayers to Your home, and since I am Your child it is also my home if I so choose to live at home.*

Hallowed be Thy name. *Here is a recognition and an expression of love, for we know that the name of the Father is holy. Yet we would ask you to see this from another vantage point. When we see and acknowledge the holiness of the name of God, we also claim the holiness of all names, all forms, all life, as the expression of God. If one were to keep this ever present in consciousness, one would begin to see and understand the power behind the words "In the beginning, God expressed and it is good." If you are a child of this Father, then the name He gave you is certainly holy.*

Thy kingdom come. *Here we ask the Father that we might see His Kingdom, and that it come into our lives.*

Thy will be done, in Earth as it is in Heaven. *In this*

62

statement, we see the recognition that "in Earth" is the Kingdom of Heaven. When you say "in Earth," you are referring to your body as it is made up of earth, not to be overshadowed by what many have confused as gross matter. You see, there is no separation in God's world. You live in an earth temple, the temple which is the dwelling place of the Most High, and you are asking that you might see and know the Source of life in yourself as you perceive it to be in Heaven. Here we also ask that it be God's will that might be expressed here in Earth, here in this temple, and that His will be expressed here as it is expressed in Heaven, the bringing of heaven in Earth.

Give us this day our daily bread. Here we ask the Father to be our food and our nourishment. "Father, please feed me, and feed me on all levels, that all of me is fed and nourished by that which gave birth to me. I want to grow and have my substance from my Father in heaven, for I have learned or will learn that what I can glean from the other kingdoms will feed me but not nourish me. I can be nourished only by Him who is my Source. And I will look to You, Father, for all my earthly and spiritual needs on all levels. And as I eat of the physical nature, I will know that it is You, Father, who feeds me through Your presence in all life."

And forgive us our trespasses, as we forgive those who trespass against us. Here we are saying, "Forgive me, Father, when I forget You and begin to worship the form, forgetting the essence and spirit that is the true experience of life in Earth. I will choose to forgive—or love, since to forgive is to love—all that is in my life, no matter what part of me I think has been trespassed against. For all of me is from the Father and all of me will respond to life as the Father would, for to forgive is to love, and to withhold forgiveness from any expression of life is to withhold love from life; and the only result one can then expect is pain. God knows no pain, as God knows only love; I am asking to live in God's knowing."

And leave (not lead) us not in temptation, but deliver us from evil. Here you are saying, "Come to me when I slip into the perception of believing I am separate from You, Father, but deliver us from evil. Save all of me, Father. Bring all of me back to truth, that all of me may live fully in Your presence and love." To think that we are separate from God is to believe in a lack of oneness and thus express discord.

For thine is the kingdom and the power and the glory forever and ever. Here you are saying, "For I know that all is the Father's kingdom, and I see that the Father is the power behind all life. I know that love is power, and I recognize that all glory is the Father's, for He is life Itself. Father, I know You will be the Kingdom forever and ever. I know I will be with You and You with me together in Your—our—kingdom for eternity. I see You, Father, in all life."

Amen. And so it is, and so it shall be.

So, Dearly Beloved, please remember that if you pray from this space and awareness, that which you ask you will surely receive. And that for which you feel a need for forgiveness will surely be washed away.
The Angels

So I say to you: Ask, and it will be given to you; search and you will find; knock, and the door will be opened to you. For the one who asks, always receives; the one who searches always finds; the one knocks will always have the door opened to him. (Luke 11:9,11)

The Truth About Meditation

Meditation is listening and receiving. To listen, it is important to relax the body, still the mind, and stop the chatter in the skull so we can distinguish the still, small voices from the cacophony that is normally present in our minds. We meditate to recover parts of ourselves we have unknowingly forgotten. We meditate to get another view of reality. In short, it's like coming home.

One of the things meditation allows us to do is complete the cycle: we relax, we ask, and then, in meditation, we listen and receive. And just as we pray constantly, we also constantly meditate, since we are also always "listening to." Once again, the question is—on what are we meditating?

The angels suggest we pay attention to what we are meditating upon as we move through the day and practice *listening to* what we are listening to. To what voices, both inside and out, do we give credence? Are they loving, gentle voices that are supportive and uplifting, and based on love, or are they loud, critical, judgmental voices that are full of fear? The loving voices nurture our growth; the fearful voices stifle it. So, as the angels often reminded us as we wrote this book, it is important to pay close attention to what we are meditating on as we move through the day—practice paying attention to exactly what you are actually listening to.

Conscious meditation helps us do this: it quiets the chatter so we can hear ourselves think. It also has a healing effect on the physical body since the more focused the attention and the calmer the mind, the slower the brain waves. Brain waves are faint electrical impulses emitted by the brain. There are four principal brain waves, all measured according to the speed of the brain's electrical impulses. What is presently interesting medical scientists are the internal psychological states and the physical states that have been found to be consistently associated with specific corresponding brain waves.

Beta is the most common brain wave experienced in normal waking hours. Measuring 13 or more cycles per second, beta is associated with focused attention and active thinking.

Alpha is a more peaceful brain wave, in which the speed of the impulse lowers to 8-12 cycles per second. Alpha is associated with relaxed awareness and internal focus, which is said to play a key role in clairvoyance, telepathy, and ESP. It is typically experienced to some degree when people relax and close their eyes and to a greater degree when we meditate. In what's known as hi-amplitude alpha—experienced in meditation—the physical body undergoes a variety of changes. The breath slows, oxygen consumption is reduced, and the blood pressure and heart rate lower. Thus, regular meditation is said to also engender a host of physical benefits as a result of this state of deep relaxation.

Theta, measured at 4-7 cycles per second, is the twilight zone between waking and sleeping. It is the brain wave that occurs when we are drowsily moving toward sleep and is often associated with dream-like images.

Delta, measuring 0-4 cycles per second, is the brain wave experienced when we are in a deep sleep.

In the past two decades, researchers have discovered that the most significant brain rhythms, in terms of human potential, are clearly alpha and theta. At the Menninger Foundation in Kansas, studies have shown that what are known as alpha-theta trains, associated with a state of drowsy reverie, are often filled with dream-like imagery and vivid visions of people and objects—known and unknown—that are often overlooked in our normal waking consciousness. Using sophisticated equipment to monitor electrical impulses in the brains of subjects in the alpha-theta trains, scientists have gathered a wealth of information about the unconscious. In fact, today it is a well-documented fact that the brilliant creativity of certain poets and scientists as well as many of the renowned mystics throughout history is linked to these dream states. Researchers now suggest that it is possible, by learning to enter into the alpha-theta state at will, to receive answers to our questions and spark creativity. It is also possible, since in the alpha-theta state we are relaxed and focused, to become sensitive to and aware of the angels as they speak to us in still, small inner voices or in actual visual images in our minds' eyes.

During meditation, listen for these very subtle celestially-inspired messages when you call on the angels. And if you pay close attention after your meditation, you will notice changes in your perception of people and events around you. The struggle and strain of painful or seemingly impossible situations often seem to lessen. Or you might experience a day filled with unexpected blessings. If you begin to see a visualization forming in your mind's eye, or hear a subtle inner voice, accept it. And if you do not hear or see anything in particular, pay close attention to the events of your day after your meditation. Learning how to hear the angels is like learning to hear or see all over again; it may take time to understand what you are hearing or seeing. What is important is that the more you meditate and focus on the various angels, the more you become familiar with the qualities and attributes of God—and thus more easily recognize them within yourself and touch them in others. Most of us are, of course, more familiar with fear than with the attributes of God. We know what fear feels like, tastes like, smells like; the angels are here to help us reverse that, to help us become more familiar with joy, peace, harmony, love, faith, forgiveness, grace, beauty, and truth. Since these are the attributes of God, and since we are made in the image of God, it naturally follows that these are the attributes of humankind. Thus, when we become more familiar with them, we learn more about ourselves. Then, when we find ourselves engulfed in confusion and pain and suffering, we can recall that familiar feeling and shift our experience in a twinkling of an eye from one of fear to one of love.

What Is Faith?

Faith, the great mother element, the dynamic, spiritual substance which fills all space, all time and composes all things is surrounding us always. We are literally immersed in it, composed of it and have complete control over it as we work in accordance with the law of the universe—the law of love—love for God, for our fellowman, for all created things and love for this infinite substance of everlasting power and intelligence as our mortal fingers reach out to take hold of it.

—Annalee Skarin, *Ye Are Gods*
The Philosophical Library, Inc., 1952

67

Faith is "the substance of things hoped for; the evidence of things unseen." It is a knowing that there is more to life than we can possibly hope to retrieve through our five senses alone. Faith is not something we have to search for; it is something that is constantly available. We simply have to choose to experience it. The angels offered an interesting slant on faith. According to the angels, faith is a direct result of the fact that life is vibration and that vibration has Universal Agreements based on love. And because life expresses as simple vibration, it actually has an invisible aura much like the etheric body that surrounds a human body. This invisible aura is the substance of life—and more specifically, love, light, and wisdom. When we become aware of this aura, we experience faith. Doubt, on the other hand, is the flip side of faith and is the substance of fear, not life. And fear is darkness, death, and illusion. F.E.A.R.: false evidence appearing real.

The bottom line is that we have a choice as to which aura to tune into. And because faith is a substance, when we become aware of the substance of faith, or the aura of life, what is found is the evidence of things unseen.

You see, either faith or doubt is always controlling our actions and directing the mind to build and create our lives. For instance, some people spend many of their waking hours musing about the "worst-case scenario"; what they are afraid of, what might happen, what could happen, what happened before. As a result of their doubts, they put their faith in what they *don't* want, rather than what they *do* want. Thus, they direct the mind to build what they don't want.

The truth is, we don't have to concern ourselves with what we don't want; we don't have to wrestle with it, psychoanalyze it, kill it. We're not responsible *to* our fears; we're only responsible *for* our fears. Being responsible *to* our doubts and fears involves constantly confronting them and scrutinizing them in analysis, or any number of methods that are presently used today to try to get a handle on our "shadow" selves. A person who is trying to be responsible *to* his doubts and fears often becomes addicted to the wrestling match for an entire lifetime.

The angels suggest that this approach serves only to keep us stuck in the substance of what we don't want to build in our lives and not present in the one moment where we can build with our faith the things we have hoped for. According to the angels, we need to be responsible *for* our doubts and fears, thus recognizing that they are there, dismissing them, and choosing to have faith. Invite the angels to help you; after all, that's what they're here for.

Keeping an Angel Journal

We suggest that you buy a special notebook just for recording your angelic experiences. Use your journal to make notes about observations and keep track of your changes as you get to know the angels—and yourself—better. Often, what happens is that, when we receive input from our celestial companions, we dismiss it as "just the imagination." Or, when we suddenly receive a flash of insight that gives us a solution to a problem, we forget that ten days before we had asked the angels for help on it. We often overlook the messages in the endless details of busy lives. If you date your notebook, however, and write what it is you have asked for—especially when you have asked for input on specific situations or for understanding or healing—and later record the results, it is often surprising to see that the angels have been working overtime and you may never have noticed.

It is also important to record the angelic encounters you might have. Whether it is a simple melodious ringing in the ear or a vision or a flash of insight on a baffling situation, or you actually see an angel, record the experience so you can look back and track your progress in the art of becoming more sensitive. Eventually, your journal may become the record of your adventures with a rather transformative group of friends.

Chapter Five

The Joy of Partnership:
Inviting the Angels Into Your Life

Dearly Beloved,
We are pleased that the Father has opened the door. We now have permission to move as close to you as possible, just short of disturbing or alarming you. The only key that remains in place is your asking; for those who call, we will come even closer; for those who ask, we will begin to blend with your thoughts and your energy systems. Let this be the time, for all is now in place.
The Angels

Angels have been influencing and guiding your life even before you took your first breath. In fact, there is not a single event in our lives that is not attended by their healing, protection, inspiration, and guidance. They are simply waiting for us to meet them as brothers and sisters, partners and co-creators so that we might learn from one another. In their presence, we catch a glimpse of what it would be like to have never left the Father's house; in our presence, they glimpse the challenges of free will choice and get to experience through us the depths of emotion, something that is not a part of their kingdom's experience. In short, the cooperation serves and benefits both kingdoms; in partnership with the Human Kingdom, angels experience life from a different perspective. In partnership with the angels, humans do too, expanding their awareness beyond material form.

When we are ready to experience the angels, the most

important first step is to simply invite them into our lives. Asking for their assistance is primary. It is a door-opener between the various kingdoms and worlds, and it gives the angels permission to assist us. You see, in the great Mystery School of Life on Planet Earth, this free will that we've been given—the ability to choose to create whatever we want to create—means that even the Creator can't interfere with our lives if we don't ask. That's why angelic messages are subtle. They allow us the opportunity to choose to listen or not to listen. After all, if they were to tell us what to do and how to do it, they would influence our ability to choose freely. Still, small voices leave us with an opportunity to decide for ourselves; and when we ask for assistance, the still, small voices have permission to become louder.

Preparing To Call on the Angels

Our request for a heart-to-heart encounter with the angels is called an *invocation*. An invocation is an invitation from the heart and a ritual that can be used to call the angelic beings into our lives as co-creators to help us create whatever we want to create in our lives.

But since the angelic realm is a "finer" or lighter vibration than what our five senses are accustomed to experiencing, when we wish to communicate with the angels it is necessary to lift our vibrations first—to literally lighten our load. We do this by releasing our fears and worries and all our worldly concerns and moving into a more relaxed state in which we can become sensitive to more subtle dimensions. This step is called *Dismissal*—releasing self from those perspectives, concepts, personal characteristics, and limited beliefs that no longer serve us. It involves recognizing all the emotional and mental baggage that we often carry with us, such as self-doubt, fear, disbelief, anxiety—all the emotions that come from a sense of unworthiness that can clog the lines of communication—and choosing to remember our true divine nature. Let go and forgive, forget, and choose to create anew.

Patience is critical. Be loving with yourself and recognize that you don't have to let go of *all* your baggage before you can communicate with your angels. You simply have to be willing to acknowledge that your baggage exists, allow it to be okay for the moment, and you will gradually move in the direction you want to be going, leaving behind all that is no longer working.

We often allow mental and emotional roadblocks to interfere with clear communication with the angels. The more we can clear these roadblocks from our minds, the less static on the lines of communication. Fears and desires that arise from the emotional body are the most common interferences with angelic communication. When, for example, we call on the angels to invoke more financial abundance into our lives but we call from a state of fear, panic, doubt, or concern, the response is limited because we are asking for one thing but dwelling on something else. The angels can't tell us what to choose; they can only assist in the creation if we allow them to assist.

Another interruption to communication with the angels occurs when we ask for help with something, yet at the same time remain particularly focused on or attached to a specific outcome—in other words, when we are having a difficult time giving up control. As a result, what we receive may be distorted because, since we have free will choice, the universe can give back to us only in direct proportion to our willingness to receive what is given. Suppose, for example, that you are involved in a difficult relationship, and, although you are asking for angelic input on what you should do, you've actually already decided what you will do. You are calling on the angels and anticipating that they will give you permission to do what you were going to do to begin with. If you become aware of a situation such as this, don't ask for answers; ask for assistance in following through with your decision. Or ask the angels that your heart's truest intention be known by the Father and ask that the information you receive be for the highest and best for all concerned. When you find yourself in a place of naïveté about what it is you want—when you drop the conditions on how you want the angels to fulfill your request—then you will receive the most powerful response.

A classic example is a friend of Thomas's who, despite his fervent invocations, was not able to shake his fear and doubt about the possibility of actually receiving what he had asked. At the time, he was living in a spiritual community and the members were preparing to leave on a tour to Egypt. He wanted to go, but he didn't have the money—so he set about invoking the money. After a few weeks of no money and no response, it was suggested that he consider what it was he was really asking for and simply ask the universe to send him to Egypt. Shortly after altering his invocation, he was given a free ticket based on his agreement to video the tour. What was required was clarity. When he became aware of his doubts and his lack of self-confidence when it came to raising lump sums of money, he realized a trip to Egypt was what he really wanted and if he continued to ask for money, his doubts would continue to prevent it from coming about.

Another roadblock to clear communication with the celestial realm occurs when we ask for clarity in a particular situation but we are afraid of, or not willing to hear, the truth. If with your free will you are not choosing to know, you are choosing to not get the Big Picture. Every situation in our lives is an opportunity to grow and evolve and expand our awareness. The more willing we are to hear what we cannot hear and to see what we cannot see, the more likely we are to grow and transform. And if we fail, or if we make wrong choices, we simply need to recognize our erroneous thinking and choose another perspective and consider how lucky we are to have experienced what we have, since it clearly brought us to the place where we are better able to make a more harmonious choice. There is no such thing as a mistake; there are only experiences, and if we don't like our experience we use our free will to change them.

The angels will not judge what we are asking for or try to distort situations to cause us to suffer or force us to learn difficult lessons. They *will* help us create what we have chosen to create, all the while nudging us subtly, lovingly, to remember who we are and the purpose of our experience here.

Still, there are probably very few of us, despite our best intentions, who do not keep spiraling back to fear and concern after giving the problem to the angels. The problem is one of habit—in this case a habitual pattern of believing in fear versus a habitual pattern of believing in love. As Pythagoras said, "habit is the greatest hindrance to growth." Think about it. How many of us seem to perpetually swing back and forth between a perspective of trust and surrender to one of fear and concern? In fact, this is why many of the great masters suggested prayer and meditation at least three times daily. This is one way to maintain a perspective of trust and surrender, to stay in an aura of faith, and to turn from the mass hallucination of fear that is, at present, very strong throughout the Earth.

Evocation: Calling Forth the Angels

An important step in contacting the angels, *evocation* is calling forth from within those qualities that we are invoking from outside of ourselves. If, as the mystics say, everything in the universe is also inside us, then it naturally follows that whatever we want to call into our lives is already available in our imagination, as well as in our very being. For example, if you wish to invoke the Archangel Michael for protection, *evoke* the feeling of being protected. Or, if you wish to invoke the Archangel Gabriel for clarity, *evoke* the feeling of absolute clarity. It is possible for all of us to evoke *all* of the qualities and attributes that we are invoking from the Angelic Kingdom. Unfortunately, not all of us have reached that level of self-knowledge and awareness.

To invoke a specific angel, call to mind a memory of a time you may have experienced that feeling or a memory of having experienced someone who emanates that quality. Evocation is how we meet the angels halfway. It puts us into alignment with what we are invoking and opens the way to experience true magic as invocation and evocation come together, and one and one becomes infinitely more than two could ever become.

And always remember to evoke a feeling of intimacy with the angels and with Source. Intimacy is the same experience as that of unconditional love—love without conditions, boundaries, selfishness, or attachment. When you then invoke the angels and ask for assistance with a feeling of intimacy, the asking is pure, making it easier for angels to assist because you are not giving them conditions and boundaries as to how you wish to receive their assistance.

Whom Are You Calling?

One of the most important steps before calling on your angels is to establish to *whom* or *what* you are directing your invocation. It is probably accurate to say that the possibilities are endless. But without exception, the angels would have you direct your invocations to the Father, the Source of limitless love. This step is very important because the process of invocation is not without its dangers. If we are not clear, we can invoke all manner of things. As Cayce said, don't be naïve enough to believe that there are not forces of darkness and beings and entities of all varieties from all possible dimensions that have an interest in retaining control and maintaining discord on the Earth. The most common example of this realm is anyone or anything who is trying to control our lives without allowing us free choice. This interference with free will is a dead give-away that something is amiss.

What are forces of darkness and why would they seek to manipulate? The notion of dark versus light fulfills the Universal Agreement of Polarity: an agreement that expresses the dual nature of life—light/dark, either/or, good/evil, God/God's shadow, etc. When the Creator created the Great Symphony, the Universal Agreement of Polarity was a physical result of God expressing as vibration. It also has a purpose, one that plays a critical role in a free will environment such as that of Earth. It helps us to develop discrimination and discernment. You see, to experience polarity is to be reminded of need—when we feel the depths of despair, we recognize a need for joy. When we experience chaos, we recognize a need for rhythm. Thus, we learn through experience. When polarities seem confusing, it is because we are experiencing them as contradiction: seeing one polarity as the truth and the other as a non-truth. When viewed from a larger perspective, what we are seeing is a one-sided view of a truth which changes according to rhythms and cycles.

The principle behind why so-called forces of darkness would seek to manipulate is that the realm of discord, or darkness, can exist only if it can coax God's children to lend their life forces to it in the form of belief, faith, or energy. In other words, if we collectively stopped believing in evil, evil would cease to exist. Forces of darkness know that if you turn to harmony, they have no more access to your power and they will withdraw.

The Purpose of Your Calling

After you have determined your request and dismissed any fears and doubts surrounding the issue, consider carefully the *motive* of your request. Invocation can be the most direct experience you will ever have, a total heart-level experience if perception is not clouded by the mind. The nature of that experience will be in direct response to your motive. The universe is so structured that if you choose truth, you will get truth—the only limit will be your ability to perceive and integrate it.

Motive is the inner urge that prompts you to act in a certain way; it is the goal of your actions, what you want to achieve. Consider, for example, an invocation by an artist to call in the angels to help him become the best artist of the century. What is his motive for wanting to see this come about? Is it a desire for pure self-expression, or is it a concern with establishing self-acceptance by becoming renowned through his work? Is it selfish or destructive, or is it for the good of all life? Not that one motive is better than the other; it's not. Some motives, however, are in harmony with the Universal Agreement that maintains that we are all one, and when we are living in harmony with that agreement—treating life and all living things as if they were all sacred members of one big family—then that agreement supports and nurtures our every move. When we have motives that arise from a belief that we are somehow special or better than others or separate from others, then we don't have the support of that agreement. What the angels are trying to convey to us is that the more we can discover and move into harmony with these Universal Agreements, the more ordered and harmonious and joyful our lives will be in all areas.

How do you know your true motive for your request? Ask yourself why you would want it, what you are going to do with it, how it benefits you, and how it benefits life in general. Then, ask for the willingness to know Truth above all else, without your own interpretations and opinions—to see the situation through the eyes of the Father. This simple request will help you gain even greater clarity since, if there are unconscious desires and fears that may be preventing you from achieving your goals, the angels will then have permission to bring them to your attention.

This is the beauty of working with the angels. It is not necessary to go through years of therapy or to spend endless hours dredging up the past in order to go forward. Ask the Father and your angelic teachers to reveal to you everything you need to know—all aspects, all levels, all dimensions of yourself. That request will call in the angels. In their environment of unconditional love and absolute forgiveness, you will begin to experience your own divine nature and the fears and concerns will begin to fall away.

The Importance of Clarity

Next, get specific about your request in terms of when, where, and how you want your response to come about, taking into consideration your beliefs about yourself and your beliefs about what is and is not possible. There are two choices: "I will generally put out to the universe what I want and I will take what I get" or "I will be specific with my request and know that the universe will also respond specifically." It's important when we invoke to be as clear as possible concerning what it is we are wishing to invoke. Life is far too responsive to not be certain.

One woman made an invocation a number of years ago saying simply, "I want to be of service." She told the universe, "Whoever needs help, please send them my way." When Thomas met her she had become a massage practitioner and had been through a series of painful relationships, both with lovers and roommates, that eventually escalated and became dangerous. Recently, she realized that the chaotic experiences of the past couple of years were a result of the universe granting her request and sending people that desperately needed help. So she modified her invocation, asking that she be sent through her mission and her work only people who, although they need help, are ready to take responsibility for healing themselves. It made a big difference in her life. Within a few weeks, she stopped attracting chaotic experiences and her relationships were a lot more satisfying.

Before you begin your invocation, identify what part of you is calling on the angels. Are you calling from your heart, your mental body, or your emotional body? When you call on the angels, you don't want to call on them from your mind, and you don't want to call from your emotions. You want to center your attention in the area of the heart and call on them from that place. Often, for example, you will notice that the heart, through a sudden intuition, may tell you one thing and the mind quite another. The heart tends to speak first, then the mind pipes in with reasons why this may not be the truth.

You see, thoughts come from the mind, which is bi-cameral, "having two branches," and thinks in dualities such as either/or, right/wrong, good/evil, should/shouldn't, can/can't—which leads to separation and fragmentation. Although this faculty was meant to provide us with a necessary frame of reference, it was not meant to provide us with a knowledge of the Big Picture; the mind is capable of producing evidence to support virtually any direction we choose to take, making it a highly unstable source of truth. And it was never designed or intended to be in charge of our lives. In fact, when used properly, the mind simply reflects the beauty of God's creativity and imagination.

Emotions are strong feelings, and, since our Creator and the angels speak to us through our heart-felt feelings, positive emotions such as love, passion, and joy are ways in which we can truly experience the presence of angels as well as the Creator. In fact, when the emotional body is experienced properly, it reflects the joy and glory of the soul. But there are also emotions that arise from the solar plexus and are based on fear, concern, and worry and are engulfed in survival. These negative emotions cloud everything we see or experience. When we are overcome with these emotions, angels have to take a step back until we finish with our particular melodrama. The analogy is the parent who wants to give guidance to the child but can't because the child is having a temper tantrum. When the child finally calms down, the parent can gently speak the truth to the child's heart.

The heart is the most powerful tool of expression that we have in human form. When open and responsive to its assigned purpose, it becomes the foundation of our lives and the director of love and truth. But remember, the heart—like the angels— just whispers its message. Yet in the whisper of the heart is where we can comprehend that we are the "child in whom God is well-pleased." And where we can hear the angels sing.

Angelic Invocation

To begin, be aware that you are sons and daughters of the most high God. And what kind of Father, what kind of God, would not allow His sons and daughters to appear before His face? Place yourself in a comfortable position, close your eyes and begin to relax. With each breath, imagine yourself entering ever more deeply into yourself. Let go of all thoughts and all the concerns of the day and allow your consciousness to begin to float. Gradually, begin to move deeper inside until you become aware of a bright light in the area of your heart. It is warm and inviting and you need to allow yourself to rest in it. Don't just imagine it. Feel yourself in the light that is within you. Be attentive to every detail of what you feel and sense. Allow yourself now to become very sensitive and very aware, and experience the feeling of, without effort, occupying this place that is quiet and where there are no thoughts. Imagine that Living Love, a being that is the essence of the highest Source you could ever imagine—whether God, Jesus Christ, Mohammed, or Buddha, it matters not—is directly in front of you. Allow yourself to experience what that feels like.

Then, picture yourself surrounded by angelic beings whom you have attracted because of your love and desire to know them. Now, according to what you are asking, call into your life one or more of the different angelic beings from the Throne of Grace—the place where God lives and from which you can call on any of the angels throughout the hierarchy.

> I call from the Throne of Grace, the Seraphim. Seraphim come to be with me, angels of love, and Cherubim come, angels of wisdom, come help me experience the qualities of love and wisdom. I also call the Great Archangels. From the East, I call Michael; be with me now and bring your enlightenment. From the South, Raphael, come and be with me and bring your passion and healing. From the West, Uriel, be with me and awaken me to the glory of Earth. From the North, Gabriel, be with me and awaken me to my purpose.

Once in the presence of the angels, ask your question or make your request. Ask them to be with you as you go about your day. Ask them to help you to have more loving relationships. Ask them to be your hands as you reach out to touch those loved ones around you. Ask them anything you want, but always thank them for being your partners in creating life more abundantly.

After your invocation is complete, thank God and thank the angels involved. In this case, thankfulness is more for you than for God or the angels. It is an acknowledgement that you are of value and worthy and capable of having anything and every-thing the universe is capable of manifesting. Then, feel an appreciation for all the blessings that are now in your life. When you appreciate, there is an instantaneous perspective shift; whatever is being appreciated seems to come alive, and ap-preciation begets joy.

Remember that this is just one way to invoke the angels. As we become more familiar with our angelic teachers, we can design our own invocations. There are no specific formulas, only different exercises or meditations that may or may not be effective. Since we are all unique expressions of one Creator, each person will find different ways of expression. What is most important is to develop a personal experiential relationship with your Source and the Angelic Kingdom, and that is something that can't be dictated by anyone other than you. It's a journey, an adventure. Some days you may hit "dry spells" when you feel as if nothing happens and no one is listening—occasionally they may last for weeks. Why this happens is difficult to say, but one thing is certain: one day, without explanation, it will "rain"—you will again feel the excitement of a spiritual com-panionship. And remember, sometimes in the midst of dry spells angels are most intensely working in your life. You are simply not in a position to realize it. So patience as well as faith is important in invocations.

Sometimes when you invoke the angels, you feel an imme-diate response. For example, a dilemma that once seemed extremely confusing suddenly makes sense. Or an answer is received either in the form of a calm knowing that something is true, or a still, small voice that answers a question. Whatever you experience, accept it and thank the angels. If there are no messages, thank them anyway and pay attention to what hap-pens throughout the remainder of the day and during the following week since you may notice a series of unusual and "miraculous" occurrences as your questions are addressed in the events of your days.

The final step after every invocation is living your life not as if your request *will* be granted, but as if it already *is*. This is the "Amen" to your invocation—the "and so it is."

Keep in mind that when you quiet your mind and invoke the angels, it's not as if you throw a switch and—*voilà!*—everything changes. Despite their winged persona, angels cannot instantly transform our lives without our permission. They can work only as fast and as completely as we will allow them. We are in control. Cooperation is the key. According to our degree of willingness, they will help us to recognize fears and accept and release limited beliefs. By inviting them into our lives, we invite situations and experiences that cause us to grow. And often this is, shall we say, strong medicine; any situation in which we do not yet have the capacity to love unconditionally will be brought into the light so we can acknowledge it, turn away, and choose to move in a new direction.

And though, like us, you may find hidden talents and abilities you might never have discovered if you hadn't called on the angels for help, you will also discover fears and addictions and all manner of hidden baggage waiting to be acknowledged and released. In every situation, the angels will lovingly encourage you to see your experience from a different perspective, bringing acceptance and compassion when you feel confused and disoriented and constantly reminding you of the importance and results of loving self. As you get to know your angelic teachers better, you can refresh yourself in the presence of their pure love and draw from that love to heal yourself and the world.

What the angels will not do is tell you what to do or judge your actions. In every situation, with every challenge, they will simply encourage you to be more loving. In fact, they are constantly reminding us that it is only through contacting heart-level feelings that the world and its people can finally experience peace.

Chapter Six

Except Ye Become
as Little Children

Dearly Beloved,
The desire that lives in your heart of hearts, that spark
which seeks to know and dream with the imagination of a
God who is loving, kind, and compassionate. This dream,
*this yearning, is **God**—alive and well and living in you. Dare*
to accept this dream for yourself personally and you accept
the God of your dreams.

The Angels

Consider the familiar Biblical story told of Jesus as He traveled through the countryside outside of Galilee with His apostles. As they walked in the heat of the midday sun, and the Master shared His teachings, suddenly He stopped to play with a group of shepherd children gathered on a hillside keeping watch over the sheep grazing quietly in the high grass.

As the Master, on hands and knees, was surrounded by giggling children and the sounds of laughter filled the air, the apostles gathered in the distance under the cool shade of an olive tree. They grew impatient and confused and a little annoyed at the One who had recently told them that He would be with them only for a short time. They were so concerned with learning Universal Law and the deep mysteries that they had a difficult time seeing this playful rabbi wasting His time with children. After all, they argued among themselves, had they not sacrificed everything to follow Him? And hadn't He promised that He would share great truths with them? And what about the schedule; surely if He continued His foolishness, they wouldn't arrive in Jerusalem as promised.

Finally, in frustration, one of the apostles had the audacity to approach the Master and say, "Why, when there are so many to teach, when there is so much to be done, why are You giving Your time among these children?"

And the Master responded, "Unless you become as one of these, you shall not enter the Kingdom of Heaven."

He didn't say it would be difficult to enter the Kingdom; He said you *cannot*. In fact, this was one of the few teachings recorded in the Bible in which He used such a strong word of warning. For instance, though He said it would be difficult for a rich man to enter the kingdom—as difficult as passing through the eye of a needle—He did not say it was impossible. Yet, here He warned the apostles that they could *not* enter the kingdom unless they became like children.

Think about it. Children have the ability to enter the Kingdom of Heaven until they are taught to abandon that part of the mind that lives in the imagination and the spirit world. That's where they dream dreams and build castles in the air— something most children are masters at experiencing. Unfortunately, this part of the mind is trained out of children by the time they reach adolescence and they are forced to become mature, concerned adults. Along the way, they lose the ability to become aware of the angels.

Think back to when you were a child. Remember those times when, alone in your room and safe under your quilt or outside exploring, you could get lost for hours in your imagination where you would create your own perfect world where anything was possible. And it wasn't at all like the rigid world of rules and responsibilities that your parents seemed to live in; whatever kind of world you wanted to create, you could; nothing was more practical or "realistic" than anything else. And when you awakened each day, you weren't burdened with responsibilities; you were free to experience whatever you wanted to experience. What's more, whatever companions you wanted to play with, you could; even angels would sometimes join you and whenever you had a question, you could ask and they would freely answer—that is, until you were interrupted by your mother calling you to dinner or homework, to a world that could never quite compare to the world of your imagination.

The Master was offering an important lesson to the apostles; as concerned, mature adults, it is easy to get lost in the intellectual part of the mind with its rational, logical, common-sense approach to life and neglect the imagination. And unless you renew this childlike part of your mind, you cannot imagine— and thus remember—the Kingdom of Heaven; as a result, you cannot create it and experience it *now*.

Imagination: Your Pathway Home

When we are children, it is easy to move to the other side of the veil and experience the Angelic Kingdom. Children haven't been inundated with beliefs and rules and responsibilities about what should and should not be. They have access to a world where anything imaginable is real; they can experience true imagination, the type of imagination that can be used as imagination was intended to be used: as a pathway to the Creator, a tool to help us experience our limitless creativity, and a way to open the doors to communicate with angels as well as with the Creator.

For many, *imagination* is a synonym for *unreal*. The dictionary defines it as the "forming of a mental image of something not present to the senses." But imagination is far more than either something not real or something not present to the five senses. It is a creative, spiritual force that has the potential to move us into a completely new future, something many of the greatest artists throughout history knew all along. Emerson, for example, called imagination a "very high sort of seeing," Coleridge called it the "living Power and prime Agent of all human perception," and Blake called God Himself "the supreme example of imaginative Being."

One of the distinguishing characteristics of the Human

Kingdom is our capacity to imagine what has never before been imagined; thus, we experience life as ever-evolving and expanding. Since all meaning in life comes from our consciousness, and all thoughts, all definitions, all perceptions, and all words come into our consciousness first as images, imagination is critical because the images we hold in our consciousness now create our experiences both now and in our future. In fact, there is nothing in our experience that wasn't first an image, and, every moment of our lives, we are either busy repeating patterns or using our imagination to create something new.

Ask yourself what you are creating in your life. Are you creating the Kingdom of Heaven in your backyard (Did you even know it was possible, or what it would feel like if it were?) or has your imagination become so stifled that you can't fathom such a thing? As we get older, the ability to imagine atrophies; we are told that dreams are a waste of time and "just our imagination." And each time the imagination is mocked or stifled, we get stuck perceiving life through the five senses alone and lose a chance to form bonds between our conscious minds and our deepest, innermost beings. The angels are here to help us reawaken those connections by reawakening our imaginations. They are here to remind us that we are not wasting time when we build castles in the sky—in fact, it is precisely by building castles in the sky that we can build a better future.

Reality or Mass Hallucination?

Consider the fact that everything we experience through our five senses, all sensory information that comes into our brain, is "made sense of" by connecting it to an image. In short, everything we see, hear, touch, taste, and feel is meaningless until the mind gives it a frame of reference. It does so by recalling past experiences and past knowledge and calling them up into visual or verbal images to establish a relationship between what is presently being experienced and what has been experienced in the past. For example, when we see the red of the rose and smell a familiar odor, we make a connection in our brains to a former experience of "rose" and determine what it is.

Consider the implications. As we mature into adulthood, we base our reality—everything we see, hear, feel, touch, and taste through our five senses—on what has been seen, heard, felt, touched, and tasted in the past. As a result, response becomes habitual. In the ordinary, concerned, mature adult mind, this way of comprehending reality is often arrived at through a plodding, step-by-step understanding of things in a linear fashion according to logic or in the context of "shoulds." Sri Aurobindo compares this way of "seeing" to a camera shutter that allows in only one image at a time. If something does not appear within the screen of the shutter, it simply does not exist in that moment—in other words, whatever we experience that does not fit into our concepts, our perspectives, our perception of reality is not taken into consideration. As a result, our imaginations become stunted and limited. Imagination becomes "fantasy": imagination distorted by false notions about reality garnered over the years from a world where pain and suffering are facts of life and hopes and dreams are often not possible. Fantasies are daydreams that we never really *expect* or intend to see happen, and, most importantly, we use them to escape from reality rather than as a tool to co-create our reality with the angels.

Shakespeare was right. Everything in our world, both inside and out, is a product of our imaginations. "The world is a dream and we are the dreamers." And imagination that is willing to entertain only borrowed ideas, narrow thoughts, and fear-based emotions creates limitation and anxiety; dreams and desires are never fulfilled. The challenge is to use the imagination to consider something new, to go beyond ordinary perceptions to *direct* perception and see life with the inquisitiveness and simplicity of a child—without expectation or limitation, without burdens and responsibilities, and with no notion whatsoever of how things are or how someone else said they should be. This is the pure imagination that is our natural state—the pure state of perception that can believe anything, do anything, and imagine anything, even something as mysterious and un-fathomable as angelic companions who are available to those who call upon them.

Pure imagination does not come from a mind that chews up what is seen as reality into separate, compartmentalized con-cepts based on what has always been and how it "should" be. It comes from a mind that is willing to set aside intellectual perspectives and past limitations and use the imagination to hear the intuition that can easily conceive of a Kingdom of Heaven here in our midst.

When we choose to use this part of our minds, we expand our boundaries and remember what to forget and what to remember. It is then possible to lift the veil and see the hosts of angels who are nudging us behind the scenes to remember our divinity—the "seed" inside us that has encoded into it the potential of who we've never *not* been.

In order to tap pure imagination, we have to open to an awareness of our true divine nature. Angels help us to remem-ber who we are. When identity is limited, imagination is im-prisoned within the confines of that limited identity; angels help free us. When we once see ourselves as we truly are, we move to the heart and tap pure imagination.

Angels: Master Teachers of the Heart

This pure imagination is something the angels hold very precious because it is the part of us that is most capable of making contact with our Creator, who wants nothing more than to become our companion. One of the ways angels assist us in renewing the childlike part of our minds is through touching our hearts. When we hear and feel what the heart communi-cates, we discover a whole new set of options and opportunities. You see, the heart knows who we are and when we listen to its still, small voice, we do too. When we don't, there is a sense of being cut off from intuition and inspiration—and fear takes over and fear engenders survival and when survival is upper-most, competition—the each-man-for-himself perspective—

becomes our primary reality. Competition for survival alters our relationship with every other living thing, since anyone other than self is potentially a threat. It also alters our relationship with God since, when the innocent, heart-centered, childlike part of the mind is abandoned, the mind arrives at its own logical, rational notion of a judgmental, condemning, unforgiving God. This particular variety of creator is merely a fantasy based on fear; the mind naturally assumes that the Creator has the same nature as we do since, after all, this is all it knows.

But the wake-up call has sounded. As the vibrational frequency of Earth accelerates and the energy increases exponentially, we are beginning to glimpse the truth—that all possibilities exist now, and each of us is powerful enough to imagine any possibility into a reality. It is more important than ever to pay attention to what we are creating with our thoughts and our imaginations. As the veil lifts, the "Grace of God delay mechanism" between what we think and what we manifest decreases. This delay mechanism has existed for our protection; if we instantly created whatever we entertained in our thoughts, we may well get ourselves into a heap of trouble. But as the vibrational frequency increases, this mechanism is changing; it's getting easier to manifest whatever we think and, if our thoughts are based in fear, it is also easier to get lost in worry and concern and consequently manifest these fears. In fact, now and in the future, every thought, every word, every deed, every desire will have a great impact on our personal lives and the world. It's therefore not a bad idea to become the masters of our thoughts so we can use our imaginations to re-create ourselves and co-create the Kingdom of Heaven on Earth.

That's why the angels are here: angels are masters at helping us master our experience by helping us become more aware of our thoughts and fears and the ways we unconsciously create circumstances we would prefer not to create. During the writing of this book, for example, the angels orchestrated an experience that perfectly illustrates this concept. It occurred on New Year's Eve, a few hours before midnight, while I was considering my dreams for 1994. As I lay alone in the dark, imagining the "perfect year" and reviewing in my mind the events of the twelve months that would soon come to an end—one of the most challenging years ever, littered with painful lessons and sheer financial disaster—I suddenly saw a vision of a giant movie screen. One by one, each of the painful circumstances of the past twelve months passed before my eyes. In an instant, I realized that every failure and every loss was my own creation—the creation of an imagination that had tended to imagine myself as not quite good enough, or not quite pure enough, or not quite blameless enough to ask for help from a God who was probably too busy to listen anyway. In each situation, I saw how my thoughts and expectations had created the events, and wherever I went, I met the worst-case scenario that I had secretly entertained—face-to-face. And though each situation had a slightly different cast of characters, each character read from the exact same script, and I was the author. In the final scene of the vision, I saw myself as a child surrounded by whole hosts of giggling angels, hovering like sisters and lovingly combing my hair. And in those few moments when the veil lifted between worlds, and I experienced the angels' brand of celestial loving, I caught a glimpse of how even the darkest of fears is simply illusion—fantasy based on non-truth.

Children Know They Are Special

Can you imagine feeling so loved and so protected and so safe in the knowledge and awareness that you are loved greatly, that fear doesn't exist? It's a vantage point that makes life infinitely easier than we may have previously imagined it could be.

While we wrote this book, this lesson was emphasized again and again by the angels. To the angels, the issue of self-worth plays a pivotal role in helping us to live our dreams. When we imagine we are less than others, or never quite good enough, we doubt ourselves and live in fear and recreate painful experiences until we finally remember who we are. If we don't remember who we are, how in heaven's name can we hope to remember our dreams? And the paradox, according to the angels, is this: "You search for who you are so you can discover your greatest dream, while your greatest dream is to discover who you are." Thus, for the angels, a primary assignment during these times is that of helping us to remember who we really are. When we do, self-worth is a given. After all, what is self-worth but the absolute confidence and faith in knowing that we are God's children. When this simple fact is remembered, self-worth and self-love are natural consequences.

Not only was self-worth a consistent lesson throughout the writing of this book for both of us, it was also our greatest stumbling block. During the times when we questioned our ability to say anything that even remotely resembled "truth," the angels simply couldn't communicate. The lines went dead, creativity came to a screeching halt, and writing a book—particularly on invisible things—seemed practically impossible. Then, after we tired of feeling like miserable failures, we got down on our knees and asked for help. Eventually, we began to get the message that *we* were the ones who were making the choice to not believe in ourselves, and thus to be miserable. Since we were the ones who chose it, we could just as easily choose something else. When we shifted our perspective, the work turned into play.

Remember Your Guardian Angel

Gently close your eyes and imagine for a moment that a splendid winged angel suddenly enters your room and sits at your feet, waiting for your acknowledgement. Just for a moment, forget all your vague notions about angels—the dazzling beings with halos who arrive with trumpets to announce momentous occasions. Just allow your imagination to wander and consider the question, "How would you *like* your angel to be?" What would he or she look like? Why would it come? And what message would it wish to convey to you at this particular time?

An Exercise From the Angels

Close your eyes and allow yourself to become still, letting all worry and concern fall away. As you move into a comfortable position, take three deep breaths. As you become more relaxed, allow your consciousness to move within self to the center of the heart. Feel your consciousness coming to rest at the heart center and from this point of balance begin to imagine a splendid angel entering your room. See this angel standing before you. How would you like it to look? Begin to create an image, while also asking for assistance from your angel to view it with your purest imagination. Call it forth. What does this heavenly presence feel like? Identify this feeling so you can begin to recognize when your angel is present. Say aloud: "I open myself to you now, giving you, my beloved guardian angel from the Throne of Grace, permission to blend with me so that I might come to know you better."

Begin to speak to your angel, just as you would to a loving friend. Ask anything you wish. Remember, there are no boundaries or limitations. What are some of the areas of your life experience where your angel could be of some assistance? Ask about specific experiences you wish to understand better or simply ask to learn more about your angel and how he or she assists you in your life.

Now take a moment and listen to the still, small voice of your guardian. Ask your angel if there is anything he or she wants to share with you in this moment. You may experience a feeling of love, or a sense of color, or a fragrance. You may hear a ringing like that of a tuning fork in your ear. You may see an image. Allow your angel to establish a connection with you. Ask for a name, if you wish. Ask your angel what you should call him or her. Try not to let the reasonable or logical part of the mind control this experience. Simply become sensitive to the angelic presence and know that your relationship will grow and change as you reawaken your imagination. Spend as much time as you can experiencing the angelic presence. When you are ready, take a few moments to thank your angel for being with you and assisting you to create whatever your heart is guiding you to experience. Before saying goodbye, tell your angel: "I want to know you better, so I might begin to build a more intimate relationship with my Source. Allow me to experience my Source through you. Thank you for your presence."

"I Remember" Exercise

One of the most powerful experiences you can have is to awaken your inherent ability to remember your identity, your nature, and from whence you came in what is termed the beginning. An exercise to assist in this is what we will call the "I Remember" exercise.

What is being called to conscious awareness is the remembrance of who you are, the remembrance of your ability to imagine and create the Kingdom of Heaven on Earth, and your remembrance of life as love.

This exercise is done by getting into a comfortable position and allowing the mind to become still and then repeating the words "I Remember." It is suggested that one might do this as often as time will permit, and always aloud if the situation permits. If you can find 20 minutes a day for 40 consecutive days without skipping a day, this experience will cause a major change in your conscious awareness, as well as in your beliefs about your true nature and identity.

Chapter Seven

Making Choices With the Angelic Kingdom

Dearly Beloved,
One of the greatest gifts the Father has blessed you with is the gift and blessing of choice. When one holds the ability of choice before oneself, allowing always the option of choice in every situation, one begins to see that life never has to be a routine or a repeat of patterns, for one can always use choice to lift oneself to the highest of expression and experience. Let it be love which guides your daily choices and watch as love lifts you up to the expression and experience of the glory and joy of life. And if you choose to allow us to be with you, you will begin to see that there is so much love in life, that fear is impossible.
The Angels

As the angels explained in The Great Symphony of Life, sound is the cause of creation. Since sound is simply vibration, all living things are, at the deepest level, vibration. What's more, all the members of all kingdoms—the Mineral Kingdom, the Plant Kingdom, the Animal, Human and Angelic Kingdoms—all have vibrational rates and frequencies that are unique to their kind and created specifically to give all members of each kingdom full opportunity to express their highest potential and thus fulfill their given assignments in the Divine Plan.

For the Mineral Kingdom, this actualization of potential will be expressed as the qualities of solidity, beauty, and physical awareness. For the Plant Kingdom, this actualization will be expressed as the qualities of beauty and sensitivity and the capacity to feel. For the Animal Kingdom, it will be expressed as the qualities of beauty and self-consciousness of feeling and thought. And for the Human Kingdom, it will be the full expression of ourselves as the Crowning Glory of all kingdoms, "made in the image and likeness of God" to be companions and co-creators with Him.

Yet, although each kingdom at a bottom-line level is striving to express and expand its highest potential, the Human Kingdom has one feature that none of the other kingdoms have been given—a feature that at various times in various ways appears to be either a blessing or a curse: an ability to choose whether we will express this potential or not. A mineral, a plant, an animal, and even an angel do not. A mineral doesn't decide whether it will become a diamond or opal or quartz crystal; it assumes whatever assignment it is given by the Source. It does not have a choice. Nor do members of the Plant Kingdom: as the poets say, "a rose is a rose is a rose." It doesn't have a choice to become a lily or a weed. Rose is the assignment. Nor do angels have choice. Angel is the assignment and it is never questioned.

In the Human Kingdom, on the other hand, we can choose to express our potential or not—and the way that we make that choice is through our expression; every expression is a choice. The truth is, we cannot become aware of our potential until we express it.

We Experience What We Express

Everyone has experienced those days that come from out of nowhere when everything seems to run like clockwork. Parking places become vacant at the most appropriate moments, a long-awaited phone call finally arrives; what is needed appears, and life seems to flow in effortless harmony. The secret lies in choice; what we have chosen to express at that moment that makes our experience of that particular day seem so perfectly orchestrated. According to the angels, what we experience is a direct result of what we express—in short, we experience what we express. In fact, this concept underlies many of the angelic messages. Often, for example, when we ask for angelic assistance in particularly challenging situations, their response is to turn the question around and ask us to consider exactly what we are choosing to express at that time that makes it *appear* to be a challenging one.

You see, one of the great cosmic jokes of all time, that all of us who choose to will eventually "get," is one that the mystics have been telling all along: everything outside of ourselves is a reflection of what is inside us. When we truly know that what we see is a result of our consciousness, we can take back our power and create what we want to create in our lives.

As the angels suggest, whatever we express, life mirrors back to us in the form of experience. In fact, our daily lives are crowded with all the teachings we will ever need to know—if only we had eyes to see and understand. When we are expressing love, people appear more loving. And although it may seem as if the love we are feeling is coming from somewhere outside of ourselves, in truth we are simply getting a taste of what we are dishing out. It's a concept that is most obvious in relationships between men and women, although it plays itself out in virtually every aspect of our lives. When we first fall in love, we find ourselves in a state of excitement and giddy anticipation. Everything seems magical and we are free, uplifted, and at our best. What is occurring is that we are *expressing* love at the moment and, as a result, experiencing love. The trap is that we often believe that the love we are experiencing is the other person's love. Thus, the beloved gets credit for the blissful experience, and, at least temporarily, our happiness and peace of mind are dependent on our lover's every move; no wonder it's called "falling in love."

But then the inevitable occurs; the beloved does something wrong. He or she no longer seems so perfect after all; suddenly love falls flat. What has actually happened is that, in the twinkling of an eye, we have made either a conscious or an

unconscious choice to withhold our love. And when we intentionally make the decision to stop expressing love, we experience
a lack of love in our lives—most commonly experienced as pain.
Normally, we blame our partners for pulling back their love, or
some of us simply give up on love altogether, deciding it's an
impossible task. What we fail to recognize is that when we
withhold our expression of love, love is withheld on all fronts. And
because love by its very nature seeks to express itself, when we
stop that expression, we cut off our life force and pain is the result.
In fact, every experience of pain can be traced to our choice of
withholding love. Here's an experience Thomas had nearly three
years ago that illustrates the concept perfectly.

Tragedy or Just Another Experience?

"One night, my wife and I were surprised to find ourselves
alone together for literally the first time in months. Our
daughter was spending the night at a friend's, and Timothy, our
14-year-old son, was out for the evening. So we decided to go
to dinner and just enjoy the freedom and each other. When we
returned home, at around eleven o'clock, the phone rang; it was
the hospital trauma unit informing us that Timothy had been
shot in the stomach and we needed to get there as soon as
possible. Halfway to the hospital, the car suddenly stopped in
the middle of the interstate, and it simply wouldn't start. We
waved down a pick-up truck and the driver took us to the
emergency room. When we arrived, Timothy was lying on a
stretcher, prepped for surgery, in shock. The doctor gave us
about two minutes with him, and then said, 'Sign these papers
so we can operate.' Six hours later, they wheeled him out. He
had tubes in both nostrils, two tubes in his mouth, and I.V.s in
his legs and hands, and he was on a respirator. Then, I waited
another six hours before he could be taken off the respirator and
another three until he started to regain consciousness.

"From the beginning of the experience, I had been calling
on the angels for guidance and understanding, and all along
they had responded, 'He's fine. Let him know he's fine.' Under

the circumstances, this was not particularly simple.

"As I was sitting quietly by his side waiting for him to wake up and thinking about what the angels had said, Timothy suddenly opened his eyes. Oddly enough, the first words that came out of his mouth were, 'The gun wasn't loaded.'

"I remember thinking, 'How fascinating; a perfect example of how the human mind absolutely refuses to be wrong. It isn't even concerned about the condition of the physical body. It just has to believe what it wants to believe about the situation and find some way to rationalize being right.' I felt like saying, 'Well, I guess we can go home then.'

"But before I could, he said, 'Am I going to live?'

"In that split second, with the feeling of the angels' presence very strong, an odd thing came out of my mouth. You know what I told him? 'What do you mean, are you going to live? You think you can get out of this Mystery School before it's time to leave? You'd be so lucky! No way; you can't die. There's nowhere to go. It's just an experience.'

"And do you know what happened? A big grin started to spread across his face and, in that instant, I truly understood the concept 'you experience what you express'—a concept the angels had been trying to convey to me for years. I suddenly understood that we don't have to create dramas and tragedies and soap operas in our lives. We have a choice. So, for the next hour, I sat with Timothy and suggested that he allow what was happening to be just another experience. You know, do your best to enjoy the tubes, the I.V.s, the catheters. Have as much fun as possible. And I was serious. Right away, one thing was blatantly clear; Timothy wasn't looking to the nurses or the doctor to gauge how he should experience it. He was looking to his parents for direction. A lot of what he was going to choose to believe about that moment was based on what he saw in our eyes; he would be looking to see 'What is your response to this situation?' So, I expressed to him that it was no big thing. A little uncomfortable—no doubt about that—but, in truth, just another experience.

"About that time, my wife arrived at the hospital. She walked into Timothy's room and started to panic and walked back out again. I followed her and said, 'What's going on?'

"She said, 'I just can't handle seeing Timothy like this.'

"My response was, 'Well, you have one of two choices. You can either go home, or you can choose to change your mind about it.'

"At first, MaryAnna wasn't really happy with my response. But all of a sudden, she realized she didn't have many options under the circumstances, and she made the choice to walk through it with him and make it experiential.

"When some of our friends came to sit with us, a few of them approached me and said, 'We're so sorry, Thomas. This is horrible. I mean, the worst thing that can ever happen to anyone is burying one of their children.'

"I said, 'Wait a minute. How did you get to the burial already? I'm not interested in burying my son. I'm interested in walking through this experience with him. I don't know what you're experiencing, but Timothy's fine. He's just going through an experience.'

"The most profound part of it all, and something that clearly demonstrates the wisdom of the concept, is that to this day Timothy can talk about that time and joke about it and it has never once been traumatic or a great big drama."

Power and Meaning Result From Choice

The angels have come to remind us that nothing—no experience—has power *over* us. We assign power to each of our experiences through our free will choice. We may determine the power and subsequently the meaning of each of our experiences from what we have learned in the past from our parents or our religion or by our cultural or educational beliefs, but the bottom line is that no experience has power *or* meaning until we choose how much power and meaning to give to it. In fact, from the most insignificant experience to the most monumental, we've been assigning life its power and meaning since the world as we know it first began. And we make these choices based on a number of factors: our experience of truth and the meaning and purpose of life, what we think we want and what will make us happy, and survival or what we think will protect us from our fears. Or we simply allow someone else to be responsible for choosing what life means to us and how much power different experiences will have in our lives. But since our choices affect every moment of our experience here, and inevitably we will have to live with the results of these choices, it is not a bad idea to get a handle on what we are choosing and why.

Choice Is a Direct Expression of Who You Are

There is nothing mysterious about the power of choice. We use it everyday. In fact, whether we are aware of it or not, we are always making choices. Sometimes they are simple either/or choices: left or right, stop or go, asleep or awake. Sometimes they are choices that are typically determined more as a result of habit than anything else: the content of our thoughts, our perspective of ourselves, our perspective of our lives. Other choices are monumental and once acted upon can alter the course of our lives forever.

The bottom line is that our choices—whether mundane or earth-shattering, conscious or unconscious—become our destiny as it plays itself out. We can choose to express love and play out our destiny joyously, or we can choose to express fear and trudge along anxious and tense, avoiding anything but the simplest of choices—despite the fact that even when we choose *not* to choose, we're making a choice. As we grow and mature, some of us eventually reach a turning point where we become more aware of how our choices are affecting our lives and decide to respond only with choices that are in our best interest. This wise approach is grounded in the clear recognition that how and what we choose carries with it certain consequences; since we must live with those consequences, it naturally follows that we should pay closer attention to what we are choosing, how we are arriving at our choices, and whether the consequences are what we originally had in mind.

Choices can be limited or unlimited—it depends on our beliefs. Some believe, for example, that it is not possible to live a fulfilling life filled with joy and abundance. Unfortunately, because of how the human character works, when we don't believe such a life is possible, we don't give ourselves permission to choose situations that will allow us to experience and express that belief—our non-belief becomes a self-fulfilling prophecy. We choose the vantage point of life as doom-and-gloom and validate fear as a very real thing with power. This outlook carries with it a belief that everything we "get" in our lives must be earned, and if by some random right move we prove that we are *worthy* of a joyful, abundant life by fulfilling our part of the bargain, even then we get what we *need* and rarely what we *want*. This is what the angels lovingly refer to as the "looking for the Garden of Eden while you're living in it" scenario; it is, as they say, a hell of an experience.

Because of the revolutionary leaps in understanding that are presently occurring, it is now possible to choose an entirely new expression and experience of life with the assistance of the angels. They have said, "The age has now come when we can acknowledge and co-create with all kingdoms and all beings and unite all as One, in direct communion with God, the holy, the good."

Angelic Assistance With Choices

Angels are master teachers when it comes to helping us make choices that serve our highest good because they have never lost their inner knowledge of God. When we develop a conscious companionship with these celestial beings, into our hearts they pour hopes and aspirations that cause us to become aware of possibilities we might never before have considered. In fact, when we begin to co-create with the angels, exciting new options appear in a myriad of forms. People enter our lives at perfect moments that offer vantage points we have never entertained. Or they open our minds to new perspectives by drawing our attention to things in our surroundings. This gift of new perspectives influences Thomas's life frequently; for example, often he'll suddenly get a notion to pull a book from his bookshelf and open it at random. Inevitably, it will speak to him, answering a question he may have been wrestling with for days. Or he will turn on the radio and find himself listening to lyrics that shift his perspective and offer an entirely new vantage point on a present challenge.

You see, the Angelic Kingdom is here to help us see life from a loftier or more enlightened perspective: a perspective in which we do not experience ourselves as separate from God or angels or, for that matter, any living thing. When we come to experience ourselves as we truly are and begin to glimpse our divine nature, choices tend to expand tenfold. Possibilities appear limitless. The angels are nudging us to remember that our Creator is not capable of withholding from us—who are made in His image—what He is, and thus what we are. But sometimes remembering who we really are and why in heaven's name we have come here appears to be a full-time job. The key is to move your conscious awareness past the chatter in the skull, beyond reason, to the heart. It is from this place that we can experience truth; the heart has an inherent awareness of who we are and that we are loved more than we can ever imagine and that we have never been, nor will we ever be, alone. And it is from this place—and only from this place—that we can make choices based on truth. When we ask the mind to cooperate and assist us in making choices from the still, small voice of the heart, we base our choices on what we honestly and sincerely wish to experience and what we have always dreamed we would express.

The heart does not live according to logic and reason. What's more, the heart is very familiar with love and, if given half a chance, can offer a virtual gold mine of inspiration on the subject. Furthermore, when we listen to the voice of the heart, we can hear the angels sing. Choices from the heart are always loving and supportive—not only of ourselves but of others. Choices based on reasons that come from the logical, rational mind are usually one-sided, often selfish, and typically arrived at according to what is most practical and how we see our life at that particular moment. Life is constantly changing, making choices from the reasoning mind highly unstable since the details of the particular scenario that the reasons are based upon will eventually change. And when the details change, the reasons change too.

The angels can help us see that life, no matter how chaotic or how frustrating or how impoverished or how limited, is *perfect exactly as it is*. They help us make peace with where we are right now. Although this may sound simplistic and at times patently absurd, it is something the angels emphasize again and again. It is very important to let life—the way you perceive it and the way you experience it in the present moment—be alright. Accept it with all of its challenges and stop resisting. When we don't accept situations or experiences, we are choosing to be in discord rather than harmony. We are confused, guilty, judgmental, remorseful, sad and heavy, when none of those feelings are necessary.

Angels Help Us Rise Above Life

When we surrender and let go in this way, we can tell the mind to stop its incessant chatter—since the chatter in the mind is a result of not accepting life as it is—and the angels can help us rise above the confusion. Only from this place of acceptance and surrender can we access choices that will contribute to our greater good—choices that will be more loving, lead to more joy and abundance, and help us experience and express who we truly are.

Normally, when we receive impressions about the life around us through the five senses, we engage our minds to form judgments about what is. This is what can be termed "looking through the glass darkly." In a state of surrender, however, we see "face-to-face"; and what is perceived through the five senses is altered. German novelist and poet Johann von Goethe described the concept of surrender best: "It is not a question of sitting down in a corner and puzzling out in one's mind something that one then considers correct. It is a question rather of making oneself ripe and letting the true judgment spring to meet one out of the facts themselves."

When the true judgment springs out of the facts, we see through the eyes of the heart.

But surrender can't be arrived at by force. We can't *make* ourselves surrender; we can only *allow* ourselves to surrender. We can't fight for peace; we can only allow peace to unfold. Surrender allows truth to be revealed from life's experiences. We disengage the mind with its judgments and opinions and choose to let life be the teacher by allowing people, things, and events speak and reveal their secrets to our hearts. Let go of how you think it should be, or how it is supposed to be, or beliefs and expectations about how you think it will turn out and choose your expression according to the essence of who you are—your "seed of contentment"—and watch your dreams come true.

Chapter Eight

Uncovering Your Hidden
Talents With the Angels

Dearly Beloved,
There is within you an expression of life and this expres-
sion is an attribute of the Most High Source. The greatest
gift you can contribute to the Earth—the Human Family and
all life—is to claim your talents and give them expression
through you. For can you see, if you choose not to express,
God cannot experience.

The Angels

The angels want us to know we *all* have something unique to contribute to life—even if we don't know what it is. All the talents we intended to express, long before any particular opportunity comes about to express them, are already designed into our DNA—we need only allow them expression.

When we asked the angels to offer their celestial viewpoint on the subject of expressing talents, one of their suggestions was to look to the holographic model—a model of how to experience life from the perspective that some suggest is the nature of truth. In fact, when a Hungarian engineer invented the notion in the 1940s, it marked the beginning of a paradigm shift—a whole new way of perceiving life and everything around us.

In a process called *laser holography*, pictures were taken by a laser beam shot at an object. When the light bounced off the object, it was picked up by a photographic plate. To view the picture, the laser beam was then shot at the photographic plate—and *voilà!*—the light that bounced off appeared in space as the object in a life-like, three-dimensional form that you could actually walk around and view from all sides. What most baffled scientists was the photographic plate. When seen with the naked eye, distinctly different patterns were visible, clearly showing the outline of the object as it was photographed from different directions. Yet when the plate was broken into hundreds of tiny pieces and the laser was shot at any one of the pieces, the picture projected into space was an exact replica of the entire image.

Suddenly science had physical proof of what the mystics had been saying all along: as above so below; as within so without; as is the macrocosm, so is the microcosm.

On a mundane level, the holographic model suggests that every question also contains within it an answer, every problem contains a solution, every beginning an end, and every potential possibility contains its actualization. According to the angels, when life is viewed through the lens of this model, everything we ever hope to become—all our dreams, and all of our talents—are already present in this moment; we simply need to become aware of them. This is a very different vantage point than the one from which we usually view our world. In our normal, linear mode of perceiving life, what we want and what we have are always separate—the end is somewhere beyond the beginning, the actualization is down the road from the dream—and it tricks us into feeling that what we want is always somewhere else and there is no guarantee that we will ever get there. In a hologram, everything that will ever be, already is. There's nowhere to go; everything potential already exists.

When we view life as a hologram, there is no more waiting or worrying where we will find what we have been searching for. There is no more blaming circumstance or feeling we'll never reach our dreams. In a hologram, it is impossible *not* to recognize our talents. The problem is our limited view of life, in which we have allowed in only certain religious, cultural, societal, and educational beliefs, not to mention a limited self-image. As a result, when we choose a means of self-expression, it is often within the confines of these viewpoints; talents are limited by background, education, religion, financial means—the list goes on and on.

The angels are here to remind us that we have trained ourselves well to believe in limitation. In a hologram, the password is "anything is possible"; the key is to believe it. Only beliefs block the expression of our talents. With our beliefs, we create our reality; we develop a belief, beliefs generate emotions, and emotions generate thought. This is the foundation upon which we act. Once we acknowledge our limiting beliefs and choose to believe anything is possible, we give ourselves permission to find opportunities to express a myriad of talents. When we eliminate what is blocking our expression, what is found is what we have long been searching for: an opportunity to express and experience God.

Believe in the Reality of Your Dreams

Visualize a hologram as a circle made up of and containing within its sphere all aspects of all creation from before the beginning of time to eternity. In the holographic model, every single manifestation of creation, every living thing in every kingdom, contains the blueprint for the whole within itself—inside a seed is the essence of a rose, inside a rose is the essence of the original Creator of that rose, expressed as beauty in the form of a fragrant flower. To the angels, the hologram is a working model of the concept of *oneness,* which is their very nature. Since they have never experienced themselves as separate from the divine Source of power, what they need is "never more than a wingspan away." What's more, since they are not separate from Source, they have never been anything other than an expression *of* Him; or more specifically, a manifestation. Their message to humankind is—"So are you."

Within each of us lies the same potential and the same limitlessness. The angels are here to help us recognize it. Often, we are aware of only a certain portion of ourselves and, likewise, only a certain portion of life. When we cut ourselves off from all other aspects of life, we cut ourselves off from the Source of that life. According to the angels, when life is experienced as a hologram, we open to all of life, and when we open to life, it opens to us. It does not have to be difficult when what we are becoming is what we have been all along.

Expressing an Attribute of the Creator

According to the angels, talents are our own unique means of expressing an attribute of God. Our assignment is to lovingly express those attributes we gravitate toward and are most familiar with—whether nursing or gardening or raising children or playing music—and to constantly refine them until they are expressed exactly as God would express them. As we express our talents, we experience God.

In fact, discovering our hidden talents is one way to prove that angels actually exist, since each and every talent is solid proof of one's ability to part the veil and invite forth the Angelic Kingdom. You see, humans are not the only intelligent life form on Earth; there is the Mineral Kingdom, the Vegetable Kingdom, and the Animal Kingdom, as well as the Angelic Kingdom, and each has intelligence. Each of these life forms also has a supervisory intelligence—a governorship—that keeps intact the thought forms that make them up. This role of governorship is carried out by the Angelic Kingdom. They also play this role for every attribute of God such as peace, joy, spontaneity, love—the list is endless. It is important to understand that, in order to experience them, we must contact their governorship. If you write or teach or garden or dance—whatever talents you choose to express—somewhere along the way you have either consciously or unconsciously (through a desire of the heart) given permission for the spirit, or an angel of that manifestation, to enter into and blend with your experience.

We cannot express an attribute of God without invoking the angel of that attribute. In the Great Symphony of Life, when the Creator manifested life, He manifested as a companion in spirit, or an angel, that is the embodiment of every expression that has ever been or will ever be. Thus, every talent we express is, on a more subtle level, an invitation to that angel to come forth. When we strum the harpsichord, we call in the Seraphim. When we play inspiring melodies on the piano, we invoke the Seraphim *and* the Cherubim. When we write, we often call on Gabriel and when we work with the Earth, we welcome Uriel.

Expressing Your Life Design

A *design* is a pattern used as a blueprint for creation. According to how you design your life, you create your destiny. Life lived without design is life lived without meaning and purpose. In many of the ancient Greek and Egyptian cultures, when a child was born, parents consulted astrologers and seers to understand the child's pre-determined life design. From an early age, the child was then given specific guidelines for work and play according to his or her strengths and always for the purpose of "nurturing forth" hidden talents. In our culture, this practice is rarely considered. Although certainly every parent wonders what his child will eventually become, little thought is given to offering avenues for expressing a specific life design. Design becomes more a matter of chance than purposeful intent.

Yet life is not created by accident, nor is it meant to be lived by accident. Life lived accidentally leads to a life without meaning. Even a rich man with all his material needs filled still has an innate longing to do something that matters. Unfortunately, many of us have forgotten this longing, leaving ourselves vulnerable to leaders, dictators, priests, and even family and friends to do our thinking, determine our values, and define success. When authority is placed outside of the self, inner guidance is often overlooked. Without guidance, it is easy to lose our bearings.

But this is changing. In this time of accelerated growth, people are taking back their authority, redefining their values, and expressing a need for work—and lives—that matter. From the vantage point of the angels, this need is the spark of God within all of us since the nature of God is creation and expression forever seeking to contribute to the expansiveness of life. When we experience this spark, we experience our true nature. And until we find some way to express this part of ourselves that wants to contribute in a harmonious way, there is a little fulfillment.

In the words of Parmahansa Yogananda, "Every human being has some spark of power by which he can create something which has not been created before." (*Where There is Light*, Self-Realization Fellowship, 1988.) When we choose to imagine and then create that "something which has not been created before," we are expressing that "something" in a unique and imaginative way. No one else will express it in quite the same way. And when we do, work becomes joyful and we blossom from our seed of contentment.

Uncovering Your Hidden Talents

All opportunities are open to you to find your unique expression of life. But it is impossible to discover that expression or talent by using only the mind. The mind is a magnificent and powerful tool, but it is also limited and not designed to make decisions. Since the mind can't function in a realm of unlimited variables, in order not to become overwhelmed, it is forced to limit possibilities. The heart, on the other hand, knows no limitation; it simply experiences God. What is important is to ask the mind to support the heart's desire and contribute to its expression by agreeing that everything needed is within reach and then look to the heart to uncover your dream.

It is a matter of recognizing the capacities you have and which ones, when expressed, will give you the greatest joy. What are your interests, your drives, your deepest inner longings? What are your strengths? You begin with an acknowledgement of yourself, recognizing that every attribute you were born with is worthwhile. Then consider that, in a hologram, there is no attribute that you could possibly need that is not latent within you.

Desire is the key. Desire is the still, small voice of the Creator nudging you toward the dream. If you have a desire to accomplish some goal, there is no question that you also have the attributes and qualities necessary to accomplish that goal—or you wouldn't desire it. Excitement is the clue, a magical sign from your higher self that allows you to know in any given moment the course of action that is in line with your higher purpose. It points you toward what is most *you.*

Give yourself a few moments to experience what would happen if you were to perceive life as a hologram. Use your imagination as a tool to discover what happens to your actions when you alter your beliefs. Imagine that you are a famous actor, for example, and you have been hired to play the lead in the life story of some heroic figure who viewed life as a hologram. Every experience he had ever had, every thought he had ever considered, every possible future he has ever imagined was available in the twinkling of an eye. Try to imagine what this person would feel when going about his day. When you begin to get a clear sense in your imagination of how that would feel, mimic it. Experience the heightened sense of awareness and the feeling that virtually anything is possible. Feel the profound sense of ease and effortlessness, the "doing without doing" that comes from knowing that everything that is ever needed is available now. When you act in a new way, in that moment you are a new person, and because you are experiencing and expressing life in a new way, you can't help but get new results.

Invoking the Angels to Discover Your Talents

The angels offered the following exercise to help you discover your hidden talents. You will need a notebook and pen and a block of uninterrupted time when you can be alone. After you have completed the following meditation, write down what you experienced.

1. Lie down in a relaxed and comfortable position. Close your eyes. Feel the presence of the angels and greet them with your heart.

2. Begin to breathe deeply and slowly. When taking a breath, fill the lower portion of the lungs first, then progressively allow the upper portion of the lungs to fill. Exhale, emptying the upper lungs first and then the lower area. Use a four-to-eight cycle, inhaling for four seconds, exhaling for eight seconds. Do not pause between the inhale and exhale; take in the breath slowly and steadily and continue the exhale immediately. Continue this for five minutes.

3. Imagine yourself in a quiet chapel deep in the woods where you have been directed to come to receive a special assignment from the angels. You are alone and feel completely safe and protected. It is dusk and, as the sun moves down below the trees, only a candle illuminates the hushed interior. You lie in the dark with a feeling of expectancy for this pivotal meeting for which you have been waiting your entire life.

4. Say aloud, "With permission of the Christ, I call forth from the Throne of Grace, the Archangel Gabriel." Imagine the luminous outline of an angel moving toward you from across the room. With each step she takes closer to you, you open your heart more completely and give the angel permission to announce your assignment. As the angel unrolls a scroll, you are without fear and listen calmly as the assignment is given. See yourself smiling as you realize you have known it all along.

5. As the angel moves back across the room and opens

the chapel door to leave you, thank it and open your eyes and return to sitting position.

6. Give yourself 15-30 minutes to write the story of this person's life from the moment of receiving the assignment until 20 years into the future. Although the "person" is actually you, write the story in the third person, as if you were telling the tale of someone else's life.

7. Answer the following questions: What was the message that this "person" was given by the angel? How did he feel when the angel spoke? When he returned to his life, how was it transformed after that moment in the chapel? What did he set out to accomplish? What were his major contributions? Describe the circumstances of his life ten, then 20 years later. What were some of the peak moments within those twenty years?

8. Look at the correlations between you and the character in your story. Was the character where you want to be? What were the character's dreams, and how were they expressed? Are they also your dreams? If so, what do you have to do to experience that future in the present moment?

When you are finished, you may have a better grasp on life as a holographic reality. Start considering it a model of how to experience life, and watch your life change for the better.

Dearly Beloved,
Allow yourself to get comfortable and begin to relax by

focusing on your breath for a moment and allowing your consciousness to move to the center of your devotion, to your heart of hearts, the point of balance within. From this point step out into a meadow, a beautiful sun-lit meadow, filled with beautiful multi-colored flowers. Smell the freshness of the flowers and watch as they dance in the breeze. Notice the blue sky and the white clouds as they float by. See the brilliant sun and feel the warmth of the sun on your face.

As you walk through this meadow, feel the grass beneath your feet, hear the sounds in your meadow, and feel the presence of your personal guardian angels as they walk with you. Notice that there is a violet flame that comes up from the earth. This is your personal violet flame of transformation. It burns away only what is past and outdated in your life, that which is no longer yours or in your best interest. Allow yourself to step into this violet flame. It will cleanse you, yet it will not consume you. Allow this flame to burn away all that is no longer the real you. Stand in this flame until it burns through you from a clouded violet to a pure violet. This is how you will know that it is complete. As the flame returns to a pure violet, it will begin to go out.

As this flame stops, you will now notice a brilliant pure white light coming down from above you, a pure white glowing, sparkling, healing, flowing, liquid light of God. Let this light begin to flow down over your entire being, washing, healing, cleansing as it fills you from your feet up to the top of your head, inside and out; a flowing, liquid, sparkling white light.

When you feel complete in this experience, step from the place in your meadow where you have your violet and white flames, and see before you a bench where your angels are waiting to assist you in making new and supportive choices in your life. Sit for a moment and share with your angelic friends what you see and ask your angels to help you expand your awareness of the choices and options available to you which you may not have noticed.

As you find the choice which is based in love and joy for you and all concerned, ask your angels to assist you in having the strength and understanding to be responsible for your choice and the ability to bring it to completion. Before leaving your meadow, thank your angels for being with you and your Source for sending the angels, and be sure to thank yourself for taking the time to see and choose that which is in your best interest and therefore all of life on Earth.

Chapter Nine

You Are the Crowning Glory

"When I consider thy heavens, the work of thy fingers, the moon and the stars, which thou hast ordained; what is man that thou art mindful of him... For thou has made him a little lower than the angels, and has crowned him with glory and honor. Thou madest him to have dominion over the works of thy hand: thou hast put all things under his feet." (Psalms 8:3-6)

Dearly Beloved,
We would share with you that the Master is here. He is in the midst of you in this very moment, standing in reverence and in prayer. We must tell you that we can see in His eyes a hope and a blessing of great joy. He waits for His blessed brothers and sisters to see and to move ever so gently to the birth of Living Love within self. Let us suggest with love and joy that His wait be short and His joy be great.
The Angels

When Thomas and I first made the decision to write this book, we began the process by making a list of chapter titles that captured the essence of the most obvious lessons the angels had been emphasizing for each of us over the years. Then one day, we did a special invocation and attunement with the Angelic Kingdom and extended an invitation to the angels to guide us and co-create with us each of the chapters and all they would contain.

Yet when it came time to write each chapter, without exception we found ourselves tongue-tied and strangely distrustful about what it was we thought we knew and if, in truth, we knew anything at all about angels and what they have to teach. Early on, however, it became increasingly clear that the angels were providing all the information we needed through our everyday experiences—that, in fact, we would not be able to simply *write* each chapter. Instead, we would have to *experience* whatever we needed to express. Our understanding couldn't be intellectual and it couldn't be a result of information gathered outside of our lives. It had to be the truth as we had experienced it. Only then could we thoroughly grasp the lesson.

Sometimes it was exhilarating since it seemed as if we were both learning and growing very quickly—as if the book were a crash-course in life; in the learning, we became privy to a glimpse of how life might be experienced in an entirely new way—a way that neither of us had ever imagined in our wildest dreams.

Other times, however, it was grueling as the intensity of the learning accelerated and each new chapter became the culmination and integration of all we had experienced up to that point. It became painfully clear that anything in our lives that was in the way of truly understanding that particular truth had to go. What was required was a direct experience beyond all beliefs and all concepts and in every dimension of consciousness. With each of the chapters, a little more was required of us: a little more commitment, a little more devotion, a little more dedication, discipline, intimacy—and above all, a little more receptivity to love. And in every moment, we had to release our need to control the outcome—even when problems remained unsolved and questions unanswered—and confront our fears of the unknown.

A Time to Claim Our True Identity

This chapter was by far the most challenging—yet, oddly enough, also the one that created the most magical and profound experiences in our lives. It required a deeper commitment than any of the others, and a decision to claim, once and for all, our true identities. We had to consider long and hard exactly what it would mean to be The Crowning Glory—"made in the image and likeness of God" with the assignment to use our creativity and imagination to co-create the Kingdom of Heaven on Earth.

That requirement transformed our lives more than any other requirement for any other chapter. And although it was often terrifying, we knew it was the greatest gift the angels had given us. It demanded of us the courage to quiet the mind and become aware of the presence of the angels constantly at work in our lives. Midway through the writing of the chapter, when the prospects of making a significant change in how we experienced life seemed more and more remote, we considered giving up. Since neither of us seemed likely to make the necessary breakthroughs that would be required to write it, it appeared that the best approach was to abandon the idea altogether, gracefully sidestep the issue of ever coming to any resolution, and find a simple, painless way to close the book.

It was in this mood of giving up while still trying to persist that, one night, something snapped. We were playing, talking about life while I fingered the keys on the piano. Suddenly, before either of us was aware of the shift, we found ourselves in the midst of discussing and clarifying the exact steps that would be required to experience oneself as The Crowning Glory. Within a few short hours, in an environment of playfulness, free from the burden of responsibility, with nowhere to go, we began to track the process that occurs when one begins to catch a glimpse of one's true divine nature.

Then, of course, having committed ourselves to writing the chapter, we had to face the necessity to experience it—simple but not an easy assignment by any stretch of the imagination.

Choice Is the Key

We discovered a deceptively simple truth: in order to become The Crowning Glory, we must choose it: take God out of some faraway heaven and allow Him into every moment of our experience—but only if it is *the* most important thing in our lives. It is not enough to simply "see" the truth; we must also be willing to experience what is seen. If we are not prepared to make God a part of every thought, every emotion, and every experience, the best approach is to remain where we are.

The choice cannot be secondary; it will require all of you. As the Biblical parable suggests, it is impossible to put new wine in old bottles "else the new wine will burst and the bottles be spilled. . ." (Luke 5:27)

Because it is a Universal Agreement that neither God nor the angels can interfere with the free will of any being unless an invitation is extended, the next step is to ask—constantly. In every moment, ask the Father to become a part of everything you do. The challenge is that, when the choice is made, it is as if we have been looking through a glass darkly and suddenly come face-to-face with a whole new way of perceiving life— one that is simultaneously exhilarating and terrifying. It requires that we go beyond what is evident to the senses and, as the angels suggest, "see" with the heart. When we do, illusions shatter. We become aware of the constant barrage of beliefs, the endless, noisy chatter that goes on and on *ad nauseum* in the mind—about who we are, where we've been, where we're going, what we should do, what we must do, what has happened in the past, and what might happen in the future—all in a feeble attempt to somehow take control of our lives.

At one point, we had to stop because the lessons and realizations we were both experiencing heightened to such a degree that neither of us had any notion of where we were going or what we might become. Often, it seemed as if all possible imbalances, all parts of our beings—body, mind, heart, and spirit—were being exposed in the light of this new way of experiencing life. Because of the speed with which we were being taught, the process was often exhausting. Some days, we would find ourselves experiencing a heightened awareness that made ordinary events and things we saw on a daily basis seem bathed in an abnormally brilliant light. Other days, we would be full of fear and secret desires to return to our former way of experiencing life, which, although not necessarily fulfilling, was at least predictable. During the week before our deadline, after we completed our normal invocation and invitation to the Angelic Kingdom, the angels showed me a vision that captured the essence of the experience. Suddenly, I saw Thomas and myself as two children—deaf, dumb, blind, and brought to our knees by life—knocking at a door marked "God's house." When He came to the door, I looked into His eyes, tears streaming down my face, and whispered, "We're ready to come home now."

The angels were conveying the importance of surrender to The Crowning Glory experience, expressed in the statement of Christ, "Not my will, Father, but thine be done." You see, we must be willing to let go of the old interpretations of life and empty ourselves of how it should be or how it could be or how it once was and open, without expectation, to what is. Simply rest in the present moment that is always overflowing with experiences chosen by our higher selves to give us exactly what we need in God's perfect timing. It requires what the angels call full-time awareness, a constant moment-to-moment choice to give our attention totally to what is occurring around us and exactly how we are choosing to respond. There cannot be an exception to this; once we choose The Crowning Glory experience, every situation and every circumstance will require it, from the mundane to the most challenging.

We discovered that, when we make this choice, we are often confronted with the very situation that we consider to be the most intolerable. As a result, there is a tendency to close the heart and retreat because we think we can't possibly handle it. The truth is, we can't but our divinity can—which is precisely why this moment contains the greatest opportunity to experience our greatest potential.

During the final stages of re-writing this chapter, Thomas had an experience that demonstrated the profundity of what can happen when we allow our divinity to deal with what would otherwise seem impossible. A 14-year-old daughter of a member of his church, along with a girlfriend, was killed in a high-speed car accident and he was called to the hospital to bless and annoint the body. It was an experience with tremendous meaning for him:

"When I received the phone call, I remember experiencing a sense of terror and inadequacy, a feeling that I couldn't handle this. 'Please God. Not a child. It's too painful—too emotional.' When I arrived at the hospital, I realized instantly that the nurses hadn't had time to prep the body; when they pulled back the sheet, everything was soaked with blood. I only remember focusing on God and asking Him to come fully into the experience. Within minutes of beginning the ceremony, I looked into the child's face and felt an overwhelming sense of love that is difficult to describe. I saw and felt incredible love pouring forth from her face, filling the room and me and all of reality. In that moment, the veil lifted and I saw the face of God and experienced a degree of compassion never before known to me. All I had ever searched for—in every experience with every teacher I had ever encountered up to that moment—I found in that one situation in which I had no choice but to surrender. Letting go of all the interpretations of the experience, I ended up in my heart and from that place saw—*knew*—in an instant that love is the very foundation of life itself. Although those words were known to me intellectually, this direct experience of seeing and feeling the truth altered everything from that moment forward. For months, even years, I had sought clarity and the ability to know God. In this moment I found what I was seeking. Yet I would never have imagined that the experience would come in the death of a precious child."

The New Conclusion is Experiential

Dearly Beloved,
The New Heaven and the New Earth is here. One can no longer speak of the coming of this New Heaven and New Earth, as it is here now, taking its form in your very midst. You are the Master Builders. If you choose to build the new, you cannot see yourself as against the old. One would do

well to simply focus on the new and build toward it with every thought, feeling, and action. It is time to rest in the faith that the new has arrived and prepare to build your dream. You may find that the New Heaven and Earth is the dream within. Always it has been inside you and now draws itself to self. Allow love to live within you; then express this love at all times for all life.

The Angels

One of the frustrations of attempting to explain the steps to The Crowning Glory experience is that it can't be understood or defined by the mind. It can be grasped only by the heart; the mind can't fathom how anything in life could possibly be so simple. What's more, it can be experienced only by being fully present in the moment. When we remain in the now, there are no beliefs or concepts with which to compare our present situation. We relax with confidence and a knowing that God is good, love is power, and truth has always been our friend. It is simply a choice of a state of awareness.

The Second Coming Has Already Begun

The Angelic Kingdom has arrived at this pivotal moment to let us know that, as we collectively prepare to experience ourselves as The Crowning Glory of all kingdoms, the pain and suffering we experience is the pain of labor. According to the angels, the Human Kingdom, and in fact all kingdoms, are pregnant, and this great birth will be the birth of the Christ Child within each of us. This is the hour long prophesied—the dawning of the Second Coming of the Christ—the fully conscious incarnation of Christ in the collective consciousness of the Earth and all of its kingdoms. In the beginning of time, long before we took our first breath, we made an agreement to experience this birth; the only step remaining is to choose it, allowing the experience to unfold. As we become more conscious and aware, we will gradually feel the force of a great

127

spiritual power and comprehend the glory of it. Christ came to Earth to prepare the Earth and humanity for this time. At his resurrection and ascension, the "Christ impulse" was introduced into the physical structure of the Earth, where it has rested as a seed for some 2000 years. Conditions are now ripe for the seed to blossom.

Angels are the midwives who have come to prepare humankind for this monumental experience. Some of the work they are doing involves moving in and through our bodies, clearing and aligning us so that collectively we can remember who we are and the purpose of our coming. In short, this alignment allows the love of God to flow through us more completely. This is the simplicity of it—and all that has ever and will ever matter. The angels remind us that the labor pains are unnecessary; they are based on a belief that something is not complete about this Earth experience. As a result, pain is experienced in an effort to somehow locate the missing element that would add meaning and purpose to life. According to the angels, the missing element is love; humans need to learn to love, to let every fiber of our beings express love in all experiences and all circumstances. To give love, to think love, to live love, to speak love, and to always to respond with love in all things and all ways.

Once we have chosen, we remain fully present in the moment; not searching through the past or distracted by some longed-for future, but present in this singular moment and then present in the next. When we are, truth will no longer be only what we think, or what we believe, or what we speak; it will be what we are.

In the midst of this great change, as we awaken to a new life, we begin to recognize that God is more than we previously imagined. The days of the vengeful God, and the punishing God, or the God who sits in judgment over our every move are over. The notion that God would allow pain and suffering to be part of the process of knowing Him or who would expect us to struggle to survive is the opinion of others who were also searching for the meaning of existence. But the search is over;

the time has come to worship a God who worships us, to recognize the love that is at the very foundation of life, and to see ourselves as He sees us: with a love that doesn't have opinions and doesn't make judgments but loves unconditionally each being in all creation. It is a love that is so vast and so magnificent that very few have ever experienced it.

The Journey Begins

Today, as we complete a book which has brought the angels into every moment of every day and night, our journey has just begun. The writing of this book and the accelerated learning that it has brought about in our lives has been a refresher course to prepare us for the real journey that begins when, the book complete, we are faced with the question of whether or not both of us will have the courage to live what the angels have taught us—in each moment and with every expression in our lives.

As we stand on the threshold of a new millennium, a time when change is on the tip of every tongue, angels have come to help all of us take this journey home by pouring into our hearts and minds the truth about who we are and the purpose of this pivotal time in our Earth's history. And though we have long thought that change must be painful, the angels gently guide us to turn our attention to what we wish to co-create and to watch the illusions of pain and limitation slowly slip from view.

It is our prayer that this book will help you do just that—that it will help you take this monumental step that is before each of us—so that, together, all of us can co-create the kingdom.

As you join us on this journey with the Angelic Kingdom, look deep inside your heart and find the willingness to see yourself as you are: "the child in whom God is well pleased."

Dearly Beloved,

You are God's blessed children. It is with great honor that we accept the assignment of assisting you. We have been with you from the beginning and will be with you forever. As you choose to let love become the foundation of your life, you will begin to realize that you will do all that love has done and more. Peace on and in Earth is the "more" of which the Master spoke. As love is born in more and more of your hearts, you will find peace will reign across the Earth. Choose to love at all times and stand in that love. If it seems to you at times that things are hard and painful, love. And if it seems to you that the Earth will be destroyed, love. And if it seems to you that life is tumultuous, love. When all seems to be lost, there is but one thing to do: stand secure in love. For Love is and darkness cannot overcome light and death cannot overcome life and fear will not overcome love. We have an unshakable trust and knowing that you will choose love. We see in your hearts that this is so. Relax into this most wonderful birth of all peace on Earth as it is in heaven. You are loved. You are blessed. You are the love for which you search. You are The Crowning Glory. You are the child in whom God is well-pleased. You are the Master Builder, building the kingdom on Earth. It is all perfect. Rest in the knowing that God is in charge. Rest in the knowing that not a sparrow will be lost. Rest in the knowing that all have been called and all will choose love in their own time and purpose. Let this knowing be your strength. Let it be your guide in all that you do.

Are you smiling? Why not?

The Angels

Chapter Ten
Angels For Daily Living

Angel Cards

Dearly Beloved,

We have created these cards for the purpose of assisting you in building a personal, experiential relationship with your angelic companions. As you build such a relationship, your awareness and understanding of the nature of your Source will gradually deepen and you will come to know God as an intimate companion and friend.

We suggest creating your personal set of angel cards using large index cards so that you will have sufficient space to make notes of your experiences or draw images that will bring to mind the specific angels.

After you have designed your cards, we suggest that you choose, in a quiet moment of the morning, one that will assist you throughout the day. This will help you in coming to know the angels and become familiar with the ways in which they guide and assist you in your work and play.

Before choosing your daily card, say a short prayer, asking your Source to send you an angel to be your companion as you go about your day. Then close your eyes and pick your card, knowing you will most certainly choose the perfect angel to be with you on that day. Read the word that is the quality or essence of your angel. Close your eyes for a moment and meditate on this word and essence. Then say a short invocation aloud to call the essence in. If, for example, you have chosen the Angel of Peace, say, "I call from the Throne of Grace the Angel of Peace to walk with me throughout the day. Shining One of Peace, come." Allow yourself to attune to this angel of Peace and begin to feel its presence, affirming aloud or to yourself, "I am with the Angel of Peace and have peace and I am peaceful throughout the day." Consider for a moment an image, a color that will allow you to associate with and feel the essence of peace. When you feel you have succeeded in attuning to your angel, further attune your mind and heart to the mind and heart of God. Now release yourself to God and your angel for this day, asking for more awareness of the quality and essence of Peace to come into your life, knowing with absolute faith that your angel will be with you and will respond. Stay aware and pay attention to the events and situations that arise. You will notice as your angel blesses you with experiences and lessons to assist you in your journey and in coming to know better the particular quality you have chosen. As your day comes to a close and you prepare for sleep, record on your angel card what you experienced or learned from your angel. Be sure to take the time to thank your angel for the day and dismiss it before retiring, unless you would like the angel to remain with you through the night. If so, dismiss the angel in your morning prayer and meditation before choosing another Angel for that day.

We suggest that you work with your angel cards in this way until you can actually distinguish individual qualities of each angel. As you do so, you will become more familiar with the qualities of your Source; and this is, of course, our purpose in coming into your life in this way. Remember, Dearly Beloved, it is a blessing and our greatest desire to be with you in this way—so please, do not hesitate to call.

Angel Card Dictionary

[On each card, write "Angel of _____" and insert one of the attributes below. Illustrate or embellish the cards if you desire.]

Abundance
Acceptance
Acknowledgement

Adventure
Atonement
Attention
Balance
Beauty
Birth
Blessing
Brotherhood
Change
Clarity
Commitment
Communication
Compassion
Cooperation
Courage
Creativity
Delight
Deliverance
Dreams
Education
Efficiency
Emergence
Encouragement
Enthusiasm
Expectancy
Expression
Faith
Flexibility
Forgiveness
Freedom
Friendship
Fulfillment

Glory
Good
Grace
Gratitude
Harmony
Healing
Honesty
Hope
Humor
Inner Authority
Inspiration
Integrity
Joy
Knowledge
Light
Love
Nourishment
Obedience
Openness
Order
Passion
Patience
Peace
Play
Potential
Power
Prayer
Purification
Purity
Purpose
Relaxation
Release

Self-Worth
Service
Simplicity
Sisterhood
Spontaneity
Strength
Surrender
Sustenance
Synthesis
Tenderness
Transformation
Truth
Understanding
Wholeness
Willingness

Meal Blessings

Dearly Beloved,
All Earth is an expression of God; therefore, you will find all food is the substance of what God is. As you take food into your body, you are taking God into your temple and building a temple with the essence and substance of God. Thus, before you eat, remember to bless your food by reminding yourself of the nature of the experience. Say, "I bless this food and see the spirit of my Source in and through it. May this food build in me the nature and expression of God. May it build and heal this temple, granting me the power to become what I rightfully should become: a child of God. Christ or Living Love demonstrated what can be done with a body built of what God is. As often as I eat I will remember Love. I Bless this food in the nature of Love. Amen."

House Blessing

"Heavenly Father and Divine Mother, we ask in this moment that You would come fully into this house-blessing experience with us, filling each of us and this house with Your Holy presence, and allow us to know and experience Your presence here.

"Now we would call forth the Holy Name and Sacred Presence of Jesus, the Christ (Living Love); come as well and fully into this experience with us in this moment. Touch our minds and our hearts that we might know the presence of love here in this house, as well as recognize and experience the love which lives inside each of us.

"We now call into this house the presence of Living Truth (not as a concept or ideal, but as a Living Being, a companion) and we ask that you become our companion here as long as we occupy this home. Make your presence known to us at all times that we might know and understand truth, and guide us in all ways.

"Now in the name and nature of love, we call from the Throne of Grace the Angelic Kingdom, the Shining Ones, to come and be with us here and assist us as we make of this house a temple. Angels of the Father come close; blend with us here that we might know you and know your wishes. Be with us in all that we do here, guide us in love and joy, teach us to know peace in this temple. We would call from the Throne of Grace a Cherubim. Holy Cherubim come, make your presence known. We ask that you would stay with us here always, guarding the thoughts and consciousness of this temple and all who might enter here. We thank you for your response and welcome your blessed presence here.

"We now welcome here any angels or spirits of the nature of divine love and joy to come and be with us as we experience life as love. Now, in closing, we dismiss any expression, thought, or being which is not in perfect harmony with the life and energies we have called here. We ask all of this in the name and nature of love. So it is spoken, and so it shall be. Amen."

House Baptism

To perform a house baptism, form a circle around the house with a group of friends (or just one or two). First bless the water. Holding the first two fingers of your right hand over the water, say these words or use your own interpretation of these thoughts.

"Element of Water—Adore thy creator—we now fill you with the power and expression of love and truth, that you transform the energy of this home into a temple of the living God, a dwelling place for the most high. Wash and cleanse this house today and what is not peace and love cleanse away. We seek this in the name and nature of love."

Then, placing your right hand on the house and your left hand up over your head, say, "Let it be known this day, that the old energy and expression of this house is dead. [Throw the water on the house.] I baptize this house in the name of The Divine Father—The Holy Mother. I call the Presence of Living Love and Truth to come and fill this Temple with Light, Love, and Wisdom. Let it be known that this Temple is now the home of God, Now and Forever. Now in the nature of Love I call from the Throne of Grace an Angel from the kingdom of Principalities. Shining One, come and enclose this temple with your guidance and protection; make of this temple a place of warmth and peace; watch over this temple and all who may come and go. So it has been spoken and so it shall be. Amen."

Angel Dictionary

[The following is a list of angel identifications of various months, astrological signs, and attributes that have been used traditionally for invocation.]

Advachiel: November, Sagittarius.

Ambriel: May, Gemini, protection, communication, clarity.

Anael: Air, healing relationships, romance, passion, Venus, Moon, sexuality, prayer, Friday.

Asmodel: April, Taurus.

Barakiel: Games, success, luck, fortune, fun, laughter.

Barbiel: October, Scorpio.

Barchiel: February, Pisces.

Chamuel: Seeking Source.

Cherubim: Express attributes of wisdom, knowledge and awareness. Because of their clear awareness, they are masters at breaking crystalized mental/emotional patterns. Throughout history, depicted as Guardians of Holy Sites. Associated with music, poetry, and art. When invoked through ceremony or through sincere desire to be clear and correct in speaking or writing, they will assist by putting their clarity and awareness behind truth.

Devas: Work with the plant life of Earth. Invoke to understand how to work and play with plants and grow gardens and discover the correct plant or herb to assist in healing. Invoke when consuming food to thank the Devas for assisting in its growth and ask that the food would nourish the physical temple.

Dominions: Enhance memory, associated with the attributes of kindness and mercy. Administrators of the Divine Plan. When one begins to see and appreciate life as a gift from Source, one is in harmony with the Dominions.

Elementals: Spirits of the elements who express and experience God through the minerals. Invoke to learn how to work with crystals and gems.

Gabriel: January, Aquarius. Said to sit on the left hand of God. Associated with truth, cleansing, and icy clarity. Archangel of the North, also associated with conception and resurrection. Called the Interpreter of Dreams and the Great Announcer. "Be Pure" are the words of Gabriel.

Hamaliel: August, Virgo.

Hanael: December, Capricorn.

Haniel: Friday, victory, Venus.

Khamael: Tuesday, Mars, associated with strength and Divine Justice.

Machidiel: March, Aries.

Metatron: Angel of all Angels, Liberator.

Michael: Wednesday, Yellow, Autumn. Archangel of the East, Michael is the spiritual force working to awaken within us the Christ consciousness that is implanted in every soul. Guardian of the Way, he stands before the Throne of the Father and comes with love to strengthen our spiritual resolve and raise our level of awareness of truth. "Love All" are the words of Michael.

Muriel: June, Cancer.

Pedael: Deliverance.

Powers: Portrayed as a valiant angel with the flaming sword of punishment in one hand and the heart of Mercy in the other. Express the attributes of justice tempered by mercy. Transformers of the duality of everyday understanding to unity with the Divine.

Principalities: Protectors of religion, inspiring and guiding decisions and presiding over nations, provinces, and rulers on Earth.

Raphael: Sunday, red, Spring, associated with passion, love, and healing. The angel of science and knowledge and guardian of creative talent. The angel of the South, the words of the angel of healing are "I Dedicate."

Raziel: Wisdom, Holy Mysteries.

Samael: Mars.

Sandalphon: Associated with glory, prayer, money, and faith that all needs will be met.

Seraphim: Express the attributes of pure love, pure warmth, and those of the Higher Mind. It is from this plane that one can hear the Divine music of all life and where musicians such as Beethoven received their inspiration. If you are feeling unloved, or in need of musical inspiration, invoke the Seraphim to charge you with love and creativity.

Sprites: Spirits of water. Invoke when showering and say, "Cleanse me this day and what is not love, wash away."

Sylphs: Spirits of air. Invoke for assistance in cleansing or clearing the air or to help with inspiration, as they are drawn to those who use their minds, particularly those in the creative arts.

Thrones: Known for the attributes of constancy and steadfastness, the Thrones condense the attributes of God into visible creation.

Tzaphiel: Thursday.

Tzaphqiel: Express the attribute of understanding, Saturday.

Uriel: Green, summer, September, Libra. The angel of the West, Uriel is the angel who inspires and conveys ideas to writers and teachers. Associated with the attributes of action, determination, force of thought. "I Serve" are the words of Uriel.

Verchiel: July, Leo.

Virtues: Known as the miracles workers, these angels make the impossible possible as they bestow blessings from on high. They are most often associated with heroes and those who struggle for good. When courage is needed, call on the Virtues.

Dearly Beloved,
If you would like to contact the authors, or if you would like a personal Guardian Angel Meditation Tape, please write to:

Thomas Keller or Deborah S. Taylor
c/o The Fellowship Center
620 14th Street
Virginia Beach, VA 23451
(804) 428-5782

Thomas Keller is an ordained minister and international lecturer and teacher on personal growth and transformation. He has been lecturing on the Angelic Kingdom for more than twelve years. He resides in Virginia Beach.

Deborah S. Taylor is a former magazine editor and newspaper columnist and an internationally recognized freelance writer. She resides in Virginia Beach.